AA MINI GUIDE

ake District

GRASMERE

Authors: Mike Gerrard and John Morrison
Art Editor: Carole Philp
Editor: Sandy Draper
Cartography provided by the Mapping Services Department of AA Publishing
Internal colour reproduction: Michael Moody

Produced by AA Publishing

Published by AA Publishing (a trading name of Automobile Association Developments Limited, whose registered office is Fanum House, Basing View, Basingstoke, Hampshire RG21 4EA; registered number 1878835).

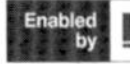

A03906

TRADE ISBN-13: 978-0-7495-5585-6
SPECIAL ISBN-13: 978-0-7495-5692-1

A CIP catalogue record for this book is available from the British Library.

Visit AA Publishing's website www.theAA.com/bookshop

Colour reproduction by Keene Group, Andover.
Printed in China by Everbest.

WETHERAL

DERWENT WATER

CONTENTS

INTRODUCTION

You can travel the world seeking beauty in a landscape, but many of the Lake District's 14 million visitors each year believe you will struggle to find somewhere as breathtakingly exquisite as this relatively small corner of northwest England. At its heart is a series of valleys (dales) cutting through an uplifted button of mountains (fells). Our very concepts of what makes a region picturesque were forged here in the late 18th century and we've been returning as gaping tourists ever since. Here are the craggy mountains, the shining lakes, the cottages to die for, the sylvan woodlands. Here, too, is the graceful osprey, the noble red deer, the impossibly cute red squirrel; even the local Herdwick sheep seem to be part of the rocky pastures they frequent. But for all that, one of Lakeland's most appealing traits is the sheer variety of its landscapes.

ASHGILL FORCE

INTRODUCTION

Despite its popularity, the Lake District retains its air of remoteness. Narrow passes, soaring mountains, plunging waterfalls and crystal-clear lakes of every shape and size create a landscape, which has inspired poets, writers and artists for more than 200 years.

In the south, the soft Silurian slate supports a series of gentle wooded undulations, giving way on their northern edge to the rough, craggy uplands of Lakeland's volcanic core. This hard stone stands tall – through the awesome power of the glaciers that shaped its valleys and mountains 10,000 years ago – leaving a range of hills higher than any other in England. These big fells (the word, like so many you'll find here, is Norse in origin) draw hundreds of thousands of walkers and climbers to the heart of the Lake District National Park, but there is plenty of space and a few minutes after escaping from your car you can find yourself alone in breathtaking countryside.

The western and eastern fringes of Lakeland have little in common apart from this sense of solitude. The west is bounded by the Irish Sea and, in some parts, an old industrial belt where lovers of industrial archaeology are perhaps the most satisfied visitors.

In the east, the Lakeland Fells give way to the green uplands of the Eden Valley, a vast unfrequented vale of pretty villages and sparkling rivers. To the north lies the border city of Carlisle, the important wildlife-rich Solway Firth and the World Heritage Site of Hadrian's Wall, stretching away over the watershed into Northumberland. The southern boundary of this delightful region is set by the treacherous shifting sands of Morecambe Bay and, for many holiday-makers from the south, the view of hills across this expanse is the first glimpse of their objective.

The Lake District has so much to offer that it is little wonder that it remains a favourite destination.

SCOTLAND
Langholm
Lockerbie
A74(M)
Dumfries
CARLISLE & BORDERLANDS
A7
A69
A689
A69
Brampton
Carlisle
Wetheral
Haltwhistle
A69
Hexham
A595
A596
Wigton
Alston
Garrigill
BASSENTHWAITE & BORROWDALE
M6
A596
Maryport
A595
Workington
Cockermouth
A66
931
Keswick
A66
Penrith
Mountains
WESTERN LAKES
A595
A66
Appleby-in-Westmorland
Whitehaven
A591
Cleator Moor
Buttermere
950
Patterdale
ULLSWATER, PENRITH & EASTERN FELLS
Brough
A66
899
Egremont
978
Grasmere
Tebay
Gosforth
A685
A595
A6
A591
M6
ESKDALE & WASDALE
Cumbrian
Windermere
Coniston
KENDAL, WINDERMERE & KENT ESTUARY
Kendal
Sedbergh
A595
A590
A595
A590
Kirkby Lonsdale
Millom
A65
Ulverston
A590
Grange-over-Sands
Dalton-in-Furness
Carnforth
Barrow-in-Furness
Morecambe
M6
Heysham
Lancaster
A65

ESSENTIAL SPOTS

If you have a little time and want to sample the best of the Lake District: visit Wordworth's Dove Cottage at Grasmere...gaze across the incomparable Tarn Hows towards Langdale Pikes...steam along the scenic Haverthwaite–Lakeside Railway...negotiate the twists and turns of Hardknott Pass...cycle around Wast Water...mingle with mountain climbers and walkers in Kendal... clamber aboard a boat for a trip on Ullswater...be enthralled by Aira Force, a series of waterfalls in a spectacular gorge.

1

1 Wast Water
The view of high fells around the head of Wast Water inspired the Lake District National Park logo, and would probably win many votes for the finest view in England.

2 Tarn Hows
Presented to the National Trust in 1930 by the Scott family, Tarn Hows is one of the most visited beauty spots in the Lake District.

3 Stockghyll Force
The 70-foot (21m) waterfall, Stockghyll Force, is one of many lovely walks that can be taken from Ambleside. The waterfall is set in lovely woodland 1 mile (1.6km) to the east of the village.

4 Grasmere

William Wordsworth lived at Grasmere with his sister, wife and young family from 1799 to 1808, writing some of his finest poetry in what he described as 'the loveliest spot that man hath ever found'.

5 Ullswater

The second largest lake in the Lake District, Ullswater, offers plenty of opportunities for watersports, such as windsurfing, sail-boarding, cruising and fishing, while the valleys and mountains provide many scenic walks and cycle rides.

6 Hardknott Roman Fort

Cumbria is criss-crossed by Roman roads. Perhaps the roughest of these highways ran from Ambleside to Ravenglass, where, Hardknott lies huddled beneath the road's wildest and highest point. The views from the fort across Duddon Valley and Coniston Fells are magnificent.

5

6

7 Bridge at Ashness

The magnificent view from here looks north across Derwent Water to the towering peaks of Skiddaw.

8 Rydal Water

Perhaps the most famous visitor to Rydal Water was William Wordsworth, who has a viewpoint named after him.

8

Day One in the Lake District

For many people a weekend break or a long weekend is a popular way of spending their leisure time. These pages offer a loosely planned itinerary designed to ensure that you make the most of your time, whatever the weather, and see and enjoy the very best the area has to offer.

Friday Night

Stay in or near Windermere – at Gilpin Lodge Country House Hotel if you can afford it! This delightful hotel, set in 20 acres (8ha) of gardens and woodland, has country-style bedrooms with some beautiful four-poster and brass beds.

Saturday Morning

Cross Windermere using the ferry service from Bowness, then follow the B5285 to visit Beatrix Potter's House, Hill Top, at Near Sawrey. Several of her 'little books' were written in this small 17th-century house. Continue northwards on the B5285 to Ambleside, one of the major centres of the Lakes and an excellent place to shop for souvenirs. If you are in Ambleside on the first Saturday in July, don't miss the rushbearing ceremony that follows in the ancient tradition of strewing the parish church floor with rushes to sweeten and purify the air for festivals and feast days. Today 'rushbearing' is a cross made of rushes or flowers and carried by the children of the parish.

RYDAL WATER

Saturday Lunch
A good place for lunch is the Drunken Duck at Barngates, which is signposted off the B5286 Hawkshead–Ambleside road. It offers a relaxed atmosphere and excellent food.

Saturday Afternoon
Drive north on the A591 for Grasmere and Keswick. Visit Rydal Mount, where William Wordsworth lived from 1813 until his death in 1850. The house is charming as it contains family portraits and many of the Wordsworth's personal possessions, and is set in beautiful gardens overlooking Rydal Water. Continue on the A591 to Grasmere. Explore the village, which has a National Park Information Centre, and then make your way to Dove Cottage and the adjacent buildings – now the Wordsworth Museum.

Saturday Night
There is plenty of accommodation in Grasmere to suit all pockets, but for something really special stay at the Wordsworth Hotel, set in lovely gardens on Stock Lane, near the church. This outstanding hotel is furnished with fine antiques and serves impressive gourmet meals.

Day Two in the Lake District

Our second and final day in the Lakes offers an excellent walk in the morning and a drive that visits a waterfall, the area's second largest lake and its highest pass. If the start of the day is wet then the morning could be spent in Keswick.

Sunday Morning

If it is wet then drive straight to Keswick. It is a natural centre for climbers, walkers and more leisurely tourists alike. If the weather is fine then it is time to discover the many delights of the Lake District on foot. There are so many fantastic walking opportunities in the Lake District that you will be spoiled for choice, but a good walk starts from the village of Elterwater, southwest of Grasmere, which leads around the superbly scenic Loughrigg Tarn.

On completing the walk, drive on the A591 to Keswick, passing the watery depths of Thirlmere on your left and the impressive heights of Helvellyn on your right.

Sunday Lunch

Keswick is the heart of the northern Lake District. You could spend a happy (wet) morning browsing round the town's tempting shops. Visit the Pencil Museum (it's more interesting than you might expect), the Cars of the Stars Motor Museum or discover the unexpected treasures of Keswick Museum and Art Gallery.

When it is time for lunch look out for The Packhorse Inn in the town centre, an attractive and comfortable pub with good food that welcomes children.

KESWICK

AIRA FORCE

Sunday Afternoon
After lunch leave Keswick on the A66 travelling east. Turn right on to the A5091 heading down towards Aira Force (National Trust), a series of waterfalls in a spectacular gorge, with an arboretum, a café and a landscaped Victorian park.

Leave the car park and travel south on the A592 along the western shore of Ullswater (the second largest lake in the Lake District National Park), passing through the popular tourist-packed villages of Glenridding and Patterdale.

Continue on the A592 to travel along spectacular Kirkstone Pass (the highest road pass in the Lake District) to return to Windermere.

Just before Windermere detour through the village of Troutbeck and visit Townend, a 17th-century wealthy yeoman farmer's house.

GRASMERE

Kendal, Windermere & Kent Estuary

AMBLESIDE

CARTMEL

CONISTON

GRANGE-OVER-SANDS

GRASMERE

GRIZEDALE FOREST

HAVERTHWAITE

HAWKSHEAD

KENDAL

KENTMERE

KIRKSTONE PASS

THE LANGDALES

LEVENS HALL

NEAR SAWREY

RYDAL MOUNT

TROUTBECK

ULVERSTON

WINDERMERE & BOWNESS-ON-WINDERMERE

INTRODUCTION

There are some fascinating towns and villages in south Lakeland, some looking out over the vast Morecambe Bay, which is fringed by delightful limestone outcrops, that are all too often overlooked by visitors as they head for the honeypots of Bowness and Windermere. The landscape here is generally greener and more intimate in character than the higher Lakeland hills, and offers delightful walking country in which you can find the 'quiet recreation' enshrined in the philosophy of the National Park.

BIRKRIGG COMMON

HOT SPOTS

Unmissable attractions

Hire a dinghy or take a more leisurely cruise at Bowness-on-Windermere... drive the spectacular Kirkstone Pass, the highest road in the Lake District, which passes through magnificent scenery...join the literary pilgrims and head to Grasmere, where Wordsworth produced some of his finest poetry... go walking in the beautiful Langdale valleys or enjoy climbs, scrambles and lowland rambles at Langdale Pikes...discover Ambleside popularised by the Lakeland poets...enjoy a drink by Coniston Water and admire its superb setting overlooked by the bulk of Old Man of Coniston...go shopping for outdoor gear or mint cake in Kendal, with its steep streets of busy shops – the essential standby for walkers and visitors on a rainy day.

1 Lake Windermere
Windermere is the largest natural freshwater lake in England. Boating and watersport facilities on the lake are excellent.

2 Dove Cottage, Grasmere
William Wordsworth found this little house while on a walking tour of the Lake District. It is a must-see for poetry lovers.

2

3

3 Great Langdale
A predominance of oak and deciduous woodlands cloak the valley flanks and bottom. The Langdale Pikes form an imposing backdrop.

AMBLESIDE

Lying at the northern tip of lake Windermere, Ambleside is a convenient base for touring the central Lakes, with Grasmere and the Langdale valleys just a short drive away. The town has adopted this role with gusto; it seems that every other shop sells walking boots and outdoor clothing.

The Romans first saw the strategic potential of this site, and built a fort they called *Galava* close to where the rivers Brathay and Rothay combine and flow into Windermere. Many centuries later, during Queen Victoria's reign, the town gained fame and prosperity through the growth of tourism.

Ambleside won its market charter in 1650, and a few buildings – including a watermill – survive from this time. However, the best-known and most photographed building in Ambleside is also the smallest: Bridge House is built on a little bridge that spans the beck of Stock Ghyll. Thought to have been built by the owners of Ambleside Hall, perhaps as a folly or apple store, Bridge House now serves as a diminutive National Trust information centre.

It is just a short walk from the centre of Ambleside to the lake at Waterhead. Like a Bowness Bay in miniature, with a short stretch of beach, dinghies for hire and ever-hungry ducks, Waterhead is a popular spot. The steamers *Swan, Tern* and *Teal* call in at Waterhead on their round-the-lake cruises.

Visit

THE ARMITT COLLECTION

Ambleside's museum was founded as a library in 1909 by the Armitt sisters. It's now a fine small museum illustrating the life and work of writers and artists such as John Ruskin, Beatrix Potter and the Collingwoods. The collection includes most of Beatrix Potter's scientific illustrations as well as pictures by artists such as William Green and J B Pyne.

AMBLESIDE

A walk in the opposite direction, following Stock Ghyll through woodland, will bring you to Stock Ghyll Force, an entrancing waterfall. 'Force' is a corruption of 'foss', the old Norse word for waterfall. Stock Ghyll once served as the heartbeat of the town when, 150 years ago, it provided power for 12 watermills

CARTMEL

First-time visitors will wonder why a village as small as Cartmel should be blessed with such a large and magnificent church. In the 12th century when Cartmel (along with Carlisle and Lanercost) was chosen as the site for an Augustinian priory, the original endowment stipulated that local people should always have the right to worship in the priory church. When the monastery itself was disbanded by the Dissolution in 1536–37 the priory church was fortunately saved.

Much of the stone from the priory was re-used to build what is now the village of Cartmel, and the only other tangible relic of monastic times is the gatehouse (in the care of the National Trust, now a heritage centre) that forms one side of the little market square. The stepped market cross stands near by, but the markets are long gone. The Cartmel of today is a pretty little village, worth exploring in its own right as well as for its gem of a church.

To the south of the village is Holker Hall, the home of the Cavendish family; allow plenty of time for your visit because there is a lot to see. The Hall itself retains the atmosphere of a family home, not least because you are free to explore the rooms unhindered by ropes and barriers. The 25 acres (10ha) of formal gardens and woodland are justifiably renowned.

Extensive outbuildings now house the Lakeland Motor Museum, where devotees of the internal combustion engine will find a collection of historic cars and other vehicles, dating from the early days of motoring to the present.

CONISTON

Overlooked by the bulk of the Old Man of Coniston, 2,627 feet (801m), and near the northern tip of Coniston Water, the village enjoys a superb setting. A little off the beaten track, Coniston caters best for those who want to explore the magnificent range of peaks that rise up behind the little grey town.

It was these mountains, and the mineral wealth they yielded, that created Coniston. While copper had been mined in this area since the Roman occupation, the industry grew most rapidly during the 18th and 19th centuries and the village expanded accordingly. The story of copper mining, slate quarrying and farming, as well as the lives of celebrities such as John Ruskin, Arthur Ransome and Donald Campbell, are told in the Ruskin Museum. Situated in Coniston since 1901, it has been recently revitalised.

A short stroll from the centre of Coniston brings you to the shore of the lake where a public slipway allows the launching of boats (no powered craft); sailing dinghies and windsurfers can be hired by the hour.

Few houses enjoy a more beautiful setting than Brantwood, in an estate on the eastern shore of the lake. From 1872 to 1900 this was the home of John Ruskin, poet, artist and social reformer, who became the most influential and controversial art critic of his time. The grounds are an attraction in their own right, and the house is filled with many of Ruskin's drawings, watercolours and other

Visit

DARING EXPLOITS

The collection of full-size replicas of their futuristic cars and boats at Holker Hall Lakeland Motor Museum incorporates an exhibition featuring the record-breaking exploits of the remarkable Campbells, Sir Malcolm (1885–1948) and his son Donald (1921–67), whose adventures on land and water thrilled the world.

items recalling the man whose ideas influenced such intellectuals as Leo Tolstoy and Mahatma Gandhi. Ruskin is buried in Coniston churchyard.

Tarn Hows, one of the most frequently visited beauty spots in the Lakes, is just a short drive from Coniston off the B5285 Hawkshead road. Just a few steps from the National Trust car park, you can gaze across the tarn, studded with islands, surrounded by conifer woodlands and rolling hills.

GRANGE-OVER-SANDS

Looking out over Morecambe Bay is the charming little resort of Grange-over-Sands, with its ornamental gardens, 1-mile-long (1.6km) promenade and relaxed ambience.

Thanks to the Gulf Stream, Grange enjoys a congenially mild climate, a factor which helps to explain why so many people find the town a pleasant place in which to spend their retirement years. Springtime is reckoned to be warmer in Grange than anywhere else in the north. Green-fingered gardeners are encouraged by the climate, and plants grow here that would be unlikely to survive elsewhere on the west coast.

GRASMERE

The village of Grasmere is central, geographically and historically, to the Lake District. Set in a valley surrounded by hills, and a short stroll from Grasmere lake, literary pilgrims have flocked here since the days when William Wordsworth's 'plain living and high thinking' produced some of the finest romantic poetry. It was during a walking tour of the Lake District, with his lifelong friend Samuel Taylor Coleridge, that Wordsworth first spied the little house that would become his home for eight of his most productive years.

Despite its size, the house came to be filled with the artistic luminaries of the day, and it was here, between 1799 and 1808, that he composed some of his best-known poems. Previously an inn (The Dove and Olive Branch), Wordsworth knew the house as Town End. It was years later, after the poet's death, that it was christened Dove Cottage. The house is open to the public, and an adjacent coach house has been converted into the Wordsworth Museum. The attached Jerwood Centre is for academic studies. It was opened in 2005 and has won awards for architecture.

By the time Wordsworth's wife, Mary, was expecting their fourth child, Dove Cottage was becoming too small. The family moved first to Allan Bank and the Rectory (both in Grasmere, and both now private homes), before making one last move to Rydal Mount.

GRIZEDALE FOREST

The Grizedale estate, situated between the lakes of Coniston Water and Windermere, was the first forest owned by the Forestry Commission to actively encourage a variety of recreational activities. The

Cats
CLIMBER
Part Five
FAMILIAR
WILD
BIRDS
JACKAL
SECURITY
GRASMERE

GRIZEDALE FOREST

forest was opened to the public in the 1960s, and Grizedale is now the largest forest in the Lake District.

The Grizedale Forest combines two roles: woodland recreation and commercial production of timber. Your first stop should be the visitor centre and the adjacent gallery, where you can get a guide to the forest's many waymarked trails. An imaginative initiative brought art into the forest. Sculptors were regularly sponsored to create artworks in woodland settings; there are now more than 80 original sculptures, to be found nestling among the trees or standing on grassy hilltops.

HAVERTHWAITE

Haverthwaite, beyond the southern tip of Windermere, is the southern terminus of the Lakeside and Haverthwaite Railway. Originally a branch of the Furness Railway, the line used to carry goods and passengers from Ulverston to connect with the Windermere steamers at Lakeside. Four passenger steamers began service in 1850; trains began running 20 years later. Passenger numbers peaked before World War I, but the story, subsequently, was sadly one of decline, curtailed services and finally, in 1967, closure.

A group of rail enthusiasts fought to buy the branch line and re-open it as a recreational line,

Activity

FELL FOOT PARK

Fell Foot Park (National Trust) offers one of the few sites on Windermere's eastern shore with public access to the water. This 18-acre (7ha) park offers safe bathing, boats for hire and space to spread a picnic blanket. A ferry runs between Fell Foot Park and Lakeside, where you will find the terminus of the restored railway and steamer berth as well as the Aquarium of the Lakes with its imaginative naturalistic displays of water and bird life in rivers, lakes and nearby Morecambe Bay.

GRIZEDALE FOREST

using steam-hauled trains. Despite many setbacks they succeeded in taking over the 3.5-mile (5.6km) stretch of line between Haverthwaite and Lakeside. The proud re-opening came in 1973; since then a full service has been maintained. As in the railway's heyday, the scenic journey can be combined with a leisurely cruise on Windermere.

Newby Bridge marks the lake's southern limit, where it drains into the River Leven. The hotel, by the bridge, with tables overlooking the river, is an ideal spot to while away an idle hour. Two miles (3.2km) from Newby Bridge is Stott Park Bobbin Mill. The 1835 building is an evocative reminder of a local industry that produced bobbins for the clattering textile mills of Lancashire.

HAWKSHEAD

Achingly picturesque, Hawkshead has suffered in recent years from the influx of visitors. Though a large car park now ensures the narrow streets comprise a car-free zone, this is no place to be on a busy bank holiday. However, the village has retained much of the charm that first endeared it to William Wordsworth, when, between 1779–87, he was a pupil at the Grammar School and lodged with Ann Tyson.

It was during his schooldays that Wordsworth developed his passion for the Lakeland hills that fuelled so much of his poetry in later life. Ann Tyson's cottage still stands, as does the school (you can see the desk on which Wordsworth carved his name).

Hawkshead is an intriguing maze of tiny thoroughfares, alleyways and courtyards. The many attractive, 17th-century whitewashed houses evidently never suffered at the hands of an unimaginative town planner, and exhibit an architectural anarchy that merely adds to the charm of the village. The 15th-century parish church boasts wall frescoes, but its main charm is its position on a grassy knoll overlooking the village.

HAWKSHEAD

A more recent attraction is the National Trust's Beatrix Potter Gallery, in the middle of the village, where you will find displays of Potter's original drawings, and information about her life as author, artist, farmer and pioneer of the conservation movement.

Hawkshead was once an important market town serving a wide area, much of it owned by the monks of Furness Abbey. Only one building now remains from monastic times: the sturdy little courthouse, just north of the village.

KENDAL

For motorists coming from the M6, the first sight of Kendal, in the valley below, means that the Lakes are 'just round the corner'. Though some motorists take the bypass, impatient to reach Bowness or Windermere, others prefer to see what Kendal has to offer. The one-way traffic system can be frustrating so it's better to explore Kendal's 'yards' or alleyways on foot than by car.

Visit

THE QUAKER TAPESTRY
Inside the Friend's Meeting House, 77 beautifully embroidered panels, the work of 4,000 men, women and children from 15 countries, illustrate the social history of the Quaker Movement.

Catherine Parr, sixth wife of Henry VIII, was born in Kendal Castle. The view repays the climb, though the castle itself is in ruins.

Near the parish church is Abbot Hall. This elegant Georgian house is now an art gallery, showing works by the many artists – including Ruskin and Constable – who were inspired by the Lakeland landscape

The Museum of Lakeland Life and Industry, also at Abbot Hall, brings recent history to life, with reconstructed shops, rooms and a farming display. The study of Arthur Ransome, author of *Swallows and Amazons* and many other children's books, has been recreated.

TO KEN

AL
BOWNESS.

At the opposite end of town, close to the railway station, the Kendal Museum has fascinating displays of geology, archaeology, natural and social history, based on the collection of 'curiosities' first exhibited by William Todhunter in 1796. He charged 'one shilling per person; children and servants 6d each'. There are displays of wildlife, both local and global (though the case of iridescent humming birds seems gross by today's standards). One of Kendal's best-known sons was Alfred Wainwright (1907–91), whose seven handwritten guides to the Lakeland hills became classics in his own lifetime. You can see Wainwright's little office in Kendal Museum, where he held the post of honorary curator for many years. A hand-drawn map reveals that his interests were already in place at the tender age of ten. However, it wasn't until he was 45 that he began the mammoth task of writing his *Pictorial Guides*, which were indispensable reading for many years to come. Other books about his beloved North Country followed, until his death in 1991.

KENTMERE

The valley of Kentmere begins at Staveley, just off the A591 between Kendal and Windermere. From Staveley the road meanders prettily along the valley bottom, northwards, never too far from the infant River Kent (which later splits the town of Kendal in two) before coming to a halt at the charming little village of Kentmere. The village church, St Cuthbert's, has a bronze memorial to Bernard Gilpin, who was born at Kentmere Hall in 1517 and eventually became Archdeacon of Durham Cathedral. From Kentmere you can continue to explore the head of the valley on foot, or take footpaths 'over the top' into either the Troutbeck valley or the remote upper reaches of Longsleddale. Be warned, you need to arrive early in the village to find a parking space at busy times.

KIRKSTONE PASS

KIRKSTONE PASS

KIRKSTONE PASS

Kirkstone Pass is, at a maximum of 1,489 feet (454m), the highest road in the Lake District, as well as one of the most spectacular. Charabancs used to labour up the long haul, from either Ambleside or Troutbeck; the Kirkstone Inn, where these roads converge, would have been a welcome sight for passengers. The pub, among one of the most isolated in Cumbria, is still a popular halt; it takes its name from the nearby Kirk Stone, which resembles a church steeple. The Kirkstone Pass continues through superb mountain scenery, before dropping down, past Brothers Water, into Patterdale.

THE LANGDALES

The Langdales are considered to be two of the most beautiful valleys in the Lake District. They are no secret, as you'll find if you drive around Great Langdale and Little Langdale on a weekend in summer. The road is very narrow; it's best to park at Skelwith Bridge or Elterwater, and tackle the area on foot. There are climbs and scrambles here to challenge the sure-footed, as well as pleasant lowland rambles if you just want to enjoy the view.

Slaters Bridge is a popular attraction in Little Langdale. It spans the River Brathay with two great slabs of slate and a stone arch. It has been speculated that the narrow arch portion of the bridge may be of Roman origin. Although a Roman road did pass through Little Langdale on its way from Hardknott to Ambleside, this is as yet unproven.

At Skelwith Bridge, where the B5343 Langdale road branches off from the A593, is Skelwith Force. The path to the waterfall continues to Elter Water, where you can enjoy one of the many views – the distinctive silhouette of the Langdale Pikes. The twin humps of Harrison Stickle (2,415 feet/736m) and Pike of Stickle (2,323 feet/708m).

Beyond the village of Chapel Stile, the Great Langdale valley opens up in spectacular fashion. The

KIRKSTONE PASS

LITTLE LANGDALE

Activity

WATER POWER OF STICKLE TARN

A popular walk in the Great Langdale valley begins at the New Dungeon Ghyll Hotel, and passes the foaming white water of Dungeon Ghyll Force before climbing steeply uphill. A surprise awaits as you reach the top – the still waters of the beautiful Stickle Tarn, with the vertiginous cliff-face of Pavey Ark behind.

Insight

GHOSTLY LEVENS HALL

Levens Hall has more than its share of ghosts. One is the Grey Lady, able to walk straight through walls, and supposed to be the ghost of a gypsy woman who was refused refreshment at the Hall. She put a curse on the house, saying that no male would inherit Levens Hall until the River Kent ceased to flow and a white deer was seen in the park. The hall did indeed pass through the female line until the birth of Alan Desmond Bagot in 1896 – an event that coincided with the river freezing over and the appearance of a white fawn.

valley floor is divided up by stone walls, dotted with farmsteads and surrounded by a frieze of mountain peaks. The valley road meanders past the Old Dungeon Ghyll Hotel. After a steep climb the road drops, with views of Blea Tarn, into the Little Langdale valley. Though not as stunning as the main valley, it is delightful and has good footpaths. It is from Little Langdale that a minor road branches west, to become first Wrynose Pass and then Hardknott Pass – exciting driving if your brakes are in good order!

LEVENS HALL

Levens Hall, just south of Kendal, is well worth a visit. The beginnings of the Hall can be traced back to a 14th-century pele tower. Typically square, with thick walls and narrow windows, the towers allowed the wealthier landowners to protect their families, livestock and servants in times of danger. The grim medieval tower at Levens was later corporated into a more elaborate Elizabethan

STOCK GHYLL, KIRKSTONE

building to create a comfortable family home. Levens Hall has passed through many hands, and now belongs to the Bagot family.

As fine as the house is, the most famous feature is outdoors. In 1688 Levens came into the possession of Colonel James Grahme [sic], who had a passion for gardening. He engaged Monsieur Beaumont to 'improve' on nature by creating a topiary garden, in which yew trees were clipped into a variety of shapes – resembling nothing so much as a surreal set of chess pieces. The designs we see today, probably the finest examples in the country, are much as they were designed three centuries ago.

Just a mile (1.6km) north of Levens Hall is Sizergh Castle, home of the Strickland family since 1239 and now owned by the National Trust. This is another building whose nucleus was a defensive pele tower that dates from the aggressive Scottish incursions of the 14th century. The house has many fine features and the gardens, with lovely views over the lower Lakeland fells, are well worth exploring.

NEAR SAWREY

Beatrix Potter first came here on holiday in 1896, fell in love with the place and used the royalties from her first book, *The Tale of Peter Rabbit* (1901), to buy Hill Top. It was in this little 17th-century farmhouse that she wrote many of her classic childrens' stories.

The success of the books allowed her to buy up farms and land: all her properties were bequeathed in 1943, to the National Trust. Her will decreed that Hill Top should remain exactly as she had known it. Visitors will recognise details from the pictures in her books and even the adjacent inn, the Tower Bank Arms, will be familiar to readers of *The Tale of Jemima Puddleduck* (1908). Disregard its unprepossessing exterior; Hill Top is chock full of memorabilia, including original drawings.

LEVENS HALL

RYDAL MOUNT

Hill Top is so popular that it is best avoided at peak holiday times. The Beatrix Potter Gallery at Hawkshead and The World of Beatrix Potter at Bowness hold lots of interest for 'Potterphiles'.

RYDAL MOUNT

By the time William Wordsworth and his family had moved to Rydal Mount, their home until the poet's death, he had already written most of the poems on which his considerable reputation now rests. The house was bought in 1969 by Mary Henderson, the poet's great great granddaughter and opened to the public the following year displaying mementos of a life devoted to literature.

While living in Rydal Mount, William Wordsworth became Distributor of Stamps for Westmorland. More propitiously he accepted the post of Poet Laureate at the age of 73, on the strict condition that he would not be have to compose verse on demand.

Visit

DORA'S FIELD

Rydal Church, partly designed by William Wordsworth, is a building worthy of closer inspection. Behind the church is Dora's Field, with its stand of oaks and pines, and full of golden daffodils between late March and early April. This piece of steeply dipping hillside beneath Rydal Mount, was dedicated by Wordsworth to his beloved daughter, Dora, who died at an early age.

In the gardens of Rydal Mount, designed by Wordsworth himself, are the terrace and shelter where many of his later poems were composed. If you visit on a spring day you will find nearby Dora's Field (bought for, and named after, the poet's daughter) awash with wild daffodils. Even those who cannot recall another line of his poetry will know about the 'host of golden daffodils', though the genesis of the poem is a walk that his sister Dorothy took along the shores of Ullswater.

TROUTBECK

With its houses spread out along narrow country lanes, without any recognisable centre, Troutbeck would hardly seem to qualify as a village. The groupings are based around a number of wells and springs, which, until recent times, were the only source of drinking water in the area. However, lovers of vernacular architecture will find a superb collection of buildings, dating from the 16th to the 19th centuries, that retain original features such as mullioned windows, heavy cylindrical chimneys and a rare example of an exposed spinning gallery. It is now designated a Conservation Area.

The best-preserved (if not the oldest) building in the Troutbeck valley is Townend, a fine example of a yeoman farmer's house. Townend offers a fascinating glimpse into what domestic life was like for Lakeland's wealthier farmers, with low ceilings, original home-carved oak panelling and furniture and stone-flagged floors.

Insight

ROMAN ROAD

The Troutbeck valley is one way that you can use to reach the spectacular Kirkstone Pass (the other route is via Ambleside). The valley was designated by the Romans to be starting point for a remarkable road, High Street, which took a, typically uncompromising, route straight across the mountain ridges that lie between the lakes of Ullswater and Haweswater.

The road is believed to have been built to link the Roman forts at Ambleside and Brougham with their port at Ravenglass on the west coast.

ULVERSTON

Ulverston, on the fringe of Morecambe Bay, is sufficiently off the beaten track to maintain an unhurried air, though Thursdays and Saturdays find the market square thronged with stalls. On top of Hoad Hill, overlooking the town, is a 90-foot (27.4m) copy of the Eddystone

TROUTBECK

Activity

ULVERSTON'S CANAL

Ulverston has the shortest canal in Britain. It is just 1 mile (1.6km) long and links the town to the sea. Built by engineer John Rennie in 1794, it represents the high point of Ulverston's iron-ore industrial history; near by were the town's foundry and blast furnace. Ships could navigate along the canal into the town to be loaded with cargoes of iron and slate.

The canal had a short working life of just 50 years, after which it was rendered redundant by the railway. Ulverston also went into decline as the iron-ore industry gradually moved to Barrow. Today the canal towpath (you can find the canal basin behind the Canal Tavern on the A590) provides a pleasant walk down to the sea.

Lighthouse. It is no help to ships, however, being a monument to Sir John Barrow, Ulverston-born in 1764. A founder member of the Royal Geographical Society, his story is told in the town's heritage centre.

In Upper Brook Street the Laurel and Hardy Museum is a honeypot for those who can't hear the Cuckoo Waltz without thinking of the bowler-hatted buffoons of the silver screen. It is not so much a museum as a haphazard collection of Laurel and Hardy memorabilia, assembled here because Stan Laurel was born in Ulverston in 1890.

No souvenir is deemed too trivial for inclusion in the displays and visitors can watch clips from some of the pair's 105 films in a tiny cinema shoehorned into a corner of the museum.

WINDERMERE & BOWNESS-ON-WINDERMERE

To many visitors, a visit to the Lakes implies nothing more strenuous than mooching around the shops of Windermere and Bowness, and a relaxing boat trip on the lake. It cannot be denied that these twin towns (almost joined into one these days) attract a disproportionate number of holiday-makers; those in search of the National Park's ethos, 'quiet recreation', should look elsewhere. Though traffic congestion is a perennial problem around the area, walkers can escape the crowds surprisingly quickly – even on the busiest of bank holidays.

The popularity of Windermere and Bowness is largely historical. Windermere is as far into the heart of the Lake District as the railway was ever driven. William Wordsworth lamented the coming of the railway; he foresaw that his beloved Lakeland would be spoiled irretrievably by an influx of visitors. Certainly the railway opened up the Lakeland landscape to working people, instead of just the well-heeled. Wordsworth was right, of course – the Lake District has changed. On the other hand, millions of people are now able to enjoy the unrivalled scenery.

It may seem a bit odd that it is Windermere, rather than Bowness at the water's edge, that takes its name from the lake. This was to provide the railway station with a more

Insight

THE NATIONAL PARK

The National Park Authority's main aims are to promote conservation, public enjoyment and the well-being of the local community. The biggest landowner within the Lake District National Park is the National Trust, which looks after large tracts of some of the finest Lakeland landscapes for the enjoyment of future generations. The Forestry Commission is another major landowner. United Utilities, too, owns three large areas within the National Park, which include Haweswater, Thirlmere and Ennerdale. Most of the land is, however, in the hands of individuals.

Visit

LAKELAND WILDLIFE OASIS

At Hale, south of Milnthorpe, working models, hands-on exhibits, computer programs and a range of live animals demonstrate the evolution of life on earth. There are free-flying butterflies, exotic vegetation, fish, reptiles, birds and mammals, plus a gift shop and a café.

LAKE WINDERMERE

appealing name; until the branch line opened in 1847, Windermere was known as Birthwaite.

Bowness offers the hordes of visitors a warm welcome, and is continually developing new enterprises for their pleasure. A few years ago it was hard to find a decent place to eat; now you can take your pick from a wide array of bistros, cafés, Indian restaurants, pizza parlours and the ever-popular fish and chip take-aways.

Insight

LAKELAND CHAR

Originally an Arctic fish, the char thrives in the cool depths of Windermere. It has long been considered a delicacy and visitors would be sure to take some potted char home with them. The fish is still served in many Lakeland hotels. The demand is satisfied by char fishermen who row their dinghies up and down the lake, patiently trailing weighted lines baited with spinners to tempt the deep-water char.

The water of England's longest lake laps gently on the beach at Bowness Bay. Swans and ducks, ell fed by visitors, enjoy an indolent lifestyle. Sleek clinker-built dinghies can be hired by the hour. The less energetic can enjoy a lake-long cruise, via Waterhead and Lakeside (linking to the steam trains of the restored Lakeside–Haverthwaite Railway), on the cruise ships Tern, Teal and Swan. Tern, with sleek lines and upturned prow, is more than a hundred years old and was once steam-powered. Since 2005 Windermere has become a more peaceful lake when the National Park Authority's hotly contested 10mph water speed limit took effect.

Opposite Bowness Bay is Belle Isle. In 1774, when notions of the 'romantic' and 'picturesque' were at their height, a Mr English built an eccentric residence. Its round design brought so much ridicule on his head (Wordsworth called it 'a pepperpot') that Mr English was prompted to sell his unusual home.

LAKE WINDERMERE

KENDAL, WINDERMERE & KENT ESTUARY

TOURIST INFORMATION CENTRES

Ambleside
Central Buildings, Market Cross.
Tel: 01539 432582

Brockhole
On the A591, Windermere.
Tel: 01539 446601

Bowness-on-Windermere
Glebe Road, Bowness Bay.
Tel: 01539 442895

Coniston
Main car park.
Tel: 01539 441533

Grange-over-Sands
Victoria Hall, Main Street.
Tel: 01539 534026

Kendal
Town Hall, Highgate.
Tel: 01539 725758

Killington Lake Services
M6 Southbound.
Tel: 01539 620138

Ulverston
Coronation Hall, County Square.
Tel: 01229 587120

Windermere
Victoria Street.
Tel: 01539 446499

PLACES OF INTEREST

Abbot Hall Art Gallery
Kirkland, Kendal.
Tel: 01539 722464

Abbot Hall Museum of Lakeland Life and Industry
Kirkland, Kendal.
Tel: 01539 722464

The Lakes Discovery Museum & the Armitt
Rydal Road, Ambleside.
Tel: 01539 431212

Beatrix Potter Gallery
Main Street, Hawkshead.
Tel: 01539 436355

Blackwell
Bowness. Tel: 01539 446139

Brantwood
Coniston. Tel: 01539 441396

Cartmel Priory
Cartmel, Grange-over-Sands.
Tel: 01539 536261

Dove Cottage
Grasmere. Tel: 01539 435544

Heron Corn Mill and Museum of Papermaking
Waterhouse Mills, Beetham.
Tel: 01539 565027

Hill Top
Near Sawrey. Tel: 01539 436269
Holker Hall and Gardens
Cark-in-Cartmel, Grange-over-Sands.
Tel: 01539 558328.
Includes the Lakeland Motor Museum.
Kendal Museum of Natural History and Archaeology
Station Road, Kendal.
Tel: 01539 721374
Laurel and Hardy Museum
4c Upper Brook Street, Ulverston.
Tel: 01229 582292
Levens Hall
Kendal. Tel: 01539 560321
Quaker Tapestry Exhibition Centre
New Road, Kendal. Tel: 01539 722975
Ruskin Museum
The Institute, Coniston.
Tel: 01539 441164
Rydal Mount
Rydal. Tel: 01539 433002
Sizergh Castle
Sizergh, nr Kendal. Tel: 01539 560070
Stott Park Bobbin Mill
Near Newby Bridge. Tel: 01539 531087
Swarthmoor Hall
Ulverston. Tel: 01229 583204
Townend
Troutbeck, Windermere.
Tel: 01539 432628
Windermere Steamboat Museum
Rayrigg Road, Windermere. Tel: 01539 445565
The World of Beatrix Potter
The Old Laundry, Bowness-on-Windermere.
Tel: 01539 488444

FOR CHILDREN

The Aquarium of the Lakes
Lakeside, Newby Bridge.
Tel: 015395 30153
Lakeside and Haverthwaite Railway
Lakeside, Newby Bridge.
Tel: 01539 531594

SHOPPING

Ambleside
Market, Wed.
Kendal
Market, Wed & Sat.
'K' Village Factory Shopping Centre.
Ulverston
Market, Thu & Sat.

LOCAL SPECIALITIES

Char

Available in Windermere.

Cumberland Sausage

Local butchers and markets.

Gingerbread

The Gingerbread Shop, Grasmere.
Tel: 01539 435428

Herdwick Lamb

Local butchers and markets.

Mills

Heron Corn Mill, Beetham, Milnthorpe.
Tel: 01539 565027

Gleaston Water Mill, Ulverston.
Tel: 01229 869244

Morecambe Bay Shrimps

Available from local fishmongers.

PERFORMING ARTS

The Brewery Arts Centre

Kendal.
Tel: 01539 725133

Coronation Hall

Ulverston.
Tel: 01229 582610

The Old Laundry

Crag Brow, Bowness-on-Windermere.
Tel: 01539 488444

SPORTS & ACTIVITIES

BOAT TRIPS

Coniston

Coniston Ferry Services, Castle Buildings, Near Sawrey, Ambleside. Tel: 01539 436216. Steam Yacht Gondola, Gondola Pier, Coniston. Tel: 01539 441288

Windermere

Windermere Lake Cruises, Lakeside, Newby Bridge, Ulverston.
Tel: 01539 531188

COUNTRY PARKS, FORESTS & NATURE RESERVES

Grizedale Forest Park, Grizedale.
Tel: 01229 860010;
www.forestry.gov.uk

CYCLE HIRE

Ambleside

Biketreks, Rydal Road.
Tel: 01539 431505

Grizedale Forest

Grizedale Mountain Bikes,
Tel: 01229 860369;
www.grizedalemountainbikes.co.uk

Staveley

Millennium Cycles, Crook Road.
Tel: 01539 821167

Windermere
Country Lanes, Windermere Railway Station. Tel: 01539 444544

CYCLE ROUTES
The W2W, Walney to Wear route to the Eden Valley and the Pennines. www.cyclingw2w.info

HORSE-RIDING

Kendal
Holmescales Riding Centre, Holmescales Farm, Old Hutton. Tel: 01539 729388

Windermere
Lakeland Pony Trekking, Limefitt Park, Troutbeck. Tel: 01539 431999; www.lakelandponytrekking.co.uk

ANNUAL EVENTS & CUSTOMS

Ambleside
Rushbearing Ceremony, first Sat in Jul.
Ambleside Sports, late Jul.
Lake District Summer Music Festival, early to mid-Aug.

Cartmel
Cartmel Steeplechases, Spring Bank Holiday.
Agricultural Show, early Aug.
Cartmel Races, Aug Bank Holiday.

Coniston
Coniston Water Festival, late May to early Jun.

Grange-over-Sands
Edwardian Festival, mid-Jun.
Lakeland Rose Show, Jul.

Grasmere
Grasmere Gala, mid-Jun.
Rushbearing Ceremony, early Aug.

Kendal
Kendal Torchlight Procession, early Sep.
Westmorland County Show, early Sep.

Kirkby Lonsdale
Lunesdale Show, mid-Aug.
Victorian Fair, early Sep.

Rydal
Rydal Sheepdog Trials, Aug.

Staveley
Lake District Sheepdog Trials, early Aug.

Ulverston
North Lonsdale Agricultural Show, late Jul.
Lantern Procession, Sep.

TEA ROOMS

The Apple Pie Eating House and Bakery
Rydal Road, Ambleside,
LA22 9AN
Tel: 015394 33679
Lakeland gingerbread is just one of the favourites here. With views over Bridge House and the hills, it's the ideal spot to enjoy the delicious treats, baked dishes or just a cappuccino.

Yew Tree Farm
Walkers' Tearoom
Coniston, LA21 8DP
Tel: 015394 41433
www.yewtree-farm.com
In a cosy farmhouse room simply furnished by Beatrix Potter herself, the Yew Tree continues a fine tradition of Cumbrian tea shops. Everything is made from scratch. Access the tea room from the public footpath that passes through the farmyard.

Hazlemere Café and Bakery
1 Yewbarrow Terrace,
Grange-over-Sands, LA11 6ED
Tel: 015395 32972
Taste more than 25 different types of tea at this traditional Victorian tea room. Local specialities include delicious Cumberland Rum Nicky and pheasant burgers.

Low Sizergh Barn Farm Shop and Tearoom
Kendal, LA8 8AE
Tel: 015395 60426
www.lowsizerghbarn.co.uk
Using the freshest local ingredients from its popular farm shop, this is a busy stop for tourists and locals.

Jumble Room
Langdale Road,
Grasmere, LA22 9SU
Tel: 015394 35188
www.thejumbleroom.co.uk
The café/restaurant, the Jumble Room creates tempting dishes from 'Thailand to Troutbeck'.

LAKESIDE & HAVERTHWAITE RAILWAY

Drunken Duck
Barngates, Ambleside, LA22 0NG
Tel: 015394 36247
www.drunkenduckinn.co.uk
This pub is popular with walkers and cyclists taking in the excellent beer and food, and the fine views.

Golden Rule
Smithy Brow, Ambleside, LA22 9AS
Tel: 015394 32257
Considered by many to be one of the few true pubs, this is a haven of good crack in front of real log fires. Beers are from Robinsons, and the food is limited, but the welcome is warm.

Old Dungeon Ghyll Hotel
Great Langdale, Ambleside, LA22 9JY
Tel: 015394 372722
www.odg.co.uk
The ODG's often full to overflowing with walkers, climbers and campers. Its reputation rests on its excellent beer and good value food. The enviable setting, below the towering Langdale Pikes, probably helps.

Mason's Arms
Strawberry Bank,
Cartmel Fell, LA11 6NW
Tel: 01539 568486
www.strawberrybank.com
Situated on a bend in a minor road as it climbs Strawberry Bank, the Mason's Arms is a popular stop on the scenic back road to Newby Bridge. There are great views from the terrace over the Winster Valley, and the interior includes a large dining area.

Black Bull
1 Yewdale Road,
Coniston, LA21 8DU
Tel: 015394 41335
www.conistonbrewery.com
Built around 400 years ago, this spacious old coaching inn is well supplied by the excellent brewery to its rear. Bar meals are pretty standard, but the restaurant offers superb dishes.

Eskdale & Wasdale

BARROW-IN-FURNESS

DUNNERDALE

ESKDALE

GOSFORTH

HARDKNOTT PASS & ROMAN FORT

MILLOM

MUNCASTER CASTLE

RAVENGLASS

WASDALE & WAST WATER

INTRODUCTION

The southern peninsulas of Cartmel and Furness attract fewer visitors but has plenty to offer them. The delightful narrow-gauge Ravenglass and Eskdale Railway, which once transported iron-ore from the Eskdale mines to the coast, now steams along the valleys of the rivers Esk and Mite carrying tourists and hikers alike, whilst unspoilt Dunnerdale is a haven for those in search of solitude amid delightful scenery. The superb coastal area offers much to walkers, birders and lovers of quiet places.

HOT SPOTS

Unmissable attractions

Discover England's highest mountain, Scafell Pike, its deepest lake, Wast Water, and plenty of opportunities for fantastic walks and cycle rides...walk in the pretty woods of Nether Wasdale or along the delightful paths that run through tranquil oak woods...look across to the expansive steel-cold screes that fan out from murky and mysterious gullies in Whin Rigg's rockfaces from the shores of Wast Water...look for purple saxifrage and alpine lady's mantle that grows in the gullies and peregrine falcons that nest on the cliff edges and precipitous crags around Buckbarrow...seek out Wasdale Head Church, one of the smallest churches in the country, it is almost lost within a tiny copse of trees...visit the isolated ruins of Hardknott Roman Fort.

1 Eskdale
These peaceful hills were once an Norman hunting preserve. Today, it is excellent walking country, with plentiful rights of way to roam.

2 Wast Water
From the Wasdale Head Road you get a grand view over Wast Water towards the screes of Yewbarow and Great Gable.

3 Muncaster Castle

Blessed with magnificent views, parts of Muncaster Castle date back to medieval times. The majority of the building is however, the result of some extensive reconstruction work which took place in 1862.

4 Hardknott Roman Fort

Situated at the western end of Hardknott Pass, This fort was built in the 2nd century AD and commands an isolated position overlooking Eskdale. The once walled and ramparted fort covered about 3 acres (1.2ha) and the ruins include fragments of watchtowers and a bath house.

4

FURNESS ABBEY

BARROW-IN-FURNESS

Even the most loyal of locals would hesitate to describe Barrow as beautiful. Until the mid-19th century there was just a tiny fishing village here, on the tip of the Furness peninsula. What made it grow at an astonishing rate were the iron- and steel-making industries, closely followed, logically, by the construction of ships.

The shipbuilding company of Vickers became almost synonymous with Barrow, and even today, long after the great days of British shipbuilding have gone, the docks and shipyards are an impressive sight. For a fascinating overview of the industry, past and present, head for one of the town's most popular attractions, the Dock Museum on North Road. Sitting astride a deep dry dock, the museum tells how, in the space of a generation, Barrow became a major force in maritime engineering. Other museum exhibits focus on older shipbuilding traditions, and the pioneers whose foresight and inventiveness helped Britain to lead the way.

A surprise awaits those visitors who drive past the museum – a road bridge links Barrow with the Isle of Walney. A cursory glance at the map shows this to be a geographic oddity shielding the tip of the Furness peninsula, and Barrow itself, from the ravages of the sea. The southern tip of the Isle of Walney is a important wildlife reserve.

Between Barrow and Dalton, in the 'Vale of Deadly Nightshade', is

Insight

FURNESS PENINSULA

The young William Wordsworth made a number of trips, on horseback, to the Furness peninsula. The red sandstone ruins of Furness Abbey inspired him to feature them in *The Prelude* and a couple of sonnets. He knew Barrow-in-Furness too, but only as a small village as yet untouched by the shipbuilding industry that transformed the town so rapidly.

Furness Abbey. Now an evocative ruin of weathered, salmon-coloured sandstone, it was, in its heyday, second in importance only to Fountains Abbey in North Yorkshire. Separated from the rest of England by sea and mountains, Furness Abbey achieved a remarkable degree of feudal independence, owning outlying farms, known as granges, as far afield as Lincolnshire and Ireland. Parts of the abbey (English Heritage) still stand to their full height, in a romantic wooded setting. The towers, arches and windows rise up in an architectural embodiment of Christian faith; the size of the community can be estimated by the fact that the monks' dormitory is 200 feet (61m) long.

The nearby village of Dalton-in-Furness, just a quiet backwater, was once the capital of Furness and the main market town for the area; but that role has passed now to Ulverston. On one side of the old market square is Dalton Castle, an uncompromisingly square sandstone building that was built by the monks of Furness Abbey as a courthouse and prison. It was restored in the 1960s, after the Castle was obtained by the National Trust from the Duke of Buccleuch.

DUNNERDALE

Dunnerdale is as delightful and unspoilt as it was when William Wordsworth first explored the valley. He knew it as the Duddon Valley, and enshrined it in a sequence of sonnets. The River Duddon rises in the hills by the Wrynose Pass, and reaches the sea at its own estuary of Duddon Sands. In between are 10 miles (16km) of the most delectable scenery – not the most dramatic, nor the most spectacular, but those who love more intimate landscapes will find Dunnerdale a delight.

The handsome little town of Broughton-in-Furness stands back from the Duddon estuary. The market square, dominated by a huge chestnut tree, boasts a stepped obelisk and a pair of stone tables

RIVER DUDDON, DUNNERDALE

that were once used to sell fish caught in the River Duddon.

From Duddon Bridge a minor road takes you up Dunnerdale. You are seldom far from the river, which is rocky and fast flowing, and the natural habitat of dippers and wagtails. There are grassy riverbanks that seem designed for spreading out a picnic blanket. Ulpha, a straggle of houses and farmsteads, is the only village of any size in the valley.

Visit

THE SWINSIDE STONE CIRCLE

The Swinside stone circle can be found on a spur of Black Combe, a little-explored fell, off the A596 between Millom and Broughton-in-Furness. Though lying on private land, the circle of 57 standing stones can be viewed from an adjacent right of way. The circle is similar in size to Castlerigg stone circle, near Keswick, though cannot boast a similarly spectacular setting.

As you continue to climb, the fields and woods give way to a more rugged landscape, as Harter Fell at 2,139 feet (652m) and the higher peaks of central Lakeland begin to dominate the view. When you reach a road junction, at Cockley Beck, your choice is between two of the most spectacular routes in the country, you can either travel west to Eskdale via the twists and turns of Hardknott Pass or east, along Wrynose Pass, and down into the breatakingly beautiful Little Langdale valley.

ESKDALE

Here is another beautiful valley that remains relatively quiet when so many other places in the Lake District are teeming with tourists and walkers. The reason is inaccessibility; to explore Eskdale most people will have to negotiate the tortuous twists, turns and hairpin bends of the Hardknott and Wrynose passes, or else take the long way round, meandering through south Lakeland.

All the better, then, for those who venture this far west, for Eskdale is well worth the effort. This is excellent walking country. For more than 30 years the Ravenglass and Eskdale Railway has enabled hikers and sightseers to venture into Eskdale without blocking up the road with their cars. This delightful narrow-gauge railway used to carry iron ore from the Eskdale mines to the coast; now the engines carry passengers up the valley. There are seven stations along the line, all offering opportunities for scenic walks with the option of taking a later train back down to Ravenglass.

The terminus, at Dalegarth, is just a short walk from Boot, a tiny village with a friendly pub, the Boot Inn. Just up the valley, the Woolpack recalls a time when this was a watering hole for the men who drove packponies heavily laden with fleeces down to the coast. Beyond a packhorse bridge spanning Whillan Beck is the delectable grouping of tiny buildings that comprise Eskdale

Activity

W2W CYCLE ROUTE

The Walney to Wear Cycle Route was inspired by the success of the Coast to Coast route, which runs from St Bees. The W2W, Sustrans regional route 20, crosses the Lake District peninsulas in easy stages to Kendal before heading up the Lune Gorge, then over the Eden Valley and across the Pennines. Its total route is 151 miles (241km) from Walney Island to Wearmouth, near Sunderland.

Mill. Cereals have been ground here since 1578, but milling ended during the 1920s. The overshot waterwheel was adapted to supply electricity to upper Eskdale; the valley was connected to the mains in 1955.

A watermill still stands beside the packhorse bridge at Boot. It was built to grind corn in 1578 and worked by successive generations of the same family for 150 years. The mill has since been restored and is now open as a museum.

GOSFORTH

Sandwiched between Wasdale and Sellafield – 'beauty and the beast', you could say – is Gosforth. Vikings, settling in the area, were gradually converted to the Christian faith, and the sandstone church at Gosforth boasts a number of artefacts dating back to this period, more than 1,000 years ago. In the churchyard is an ancient Viking cross that is 14 feet (4.3m) high, the tallest of its kind in England, and so slender that the wonder is that it has survived intact. Intricate engravings on all four sides of the cross combines pagan Viking legends with Christian teaching.

Another ancient cross in the churchyard was converted, in a fit of official vandalism two centuries ago, into a sundial. Other relics, now displayed inside the church, fared better: the Fishing Stone and a pair of hogback tombstones are potent symbols of the coming together, many centuries ago, of two disparate cultures of worship.

HARDKNOTT ROMAN FORT

HARDKNOTT PASS & ROMAN FORT

When you gaze down from the remains of the fort at the western end of the twists and turns of the Hardknott Pass (1,291 feet/393m) it is easy to see why the Romans chose this site. Hardknott Castle Roman Fort (owned by English Heritage) enjoys a commanding position down into the green valley of Eskdale. Attacks from three sides were impossible and a trench forestalled attacks from the east.

Roman soldiers were garrisoned here to safeguard the road they had built to link the fort at Ambleside and the port of Ravenglass. Preferring to take the most direct route, they drove their road over the most difficult terrain through Hardknott and Wrynose passes.

Despite the wonderful views, the Roman soldiers must have regarded isolated, windswept *Mediobogdum* as an unglamorous posting. The perimeter wall is of typical playing-card shape and the ruins are still impressive. The soldiers drilled on a flat parade ground near by. The bathhouse would have been one of their few comforts.

Hardknott Pass, rising 1,000 feet (305m) out of Eskdale in little more than a mile (1.6km), is one of the most spectacular roads in the country; a few of the hairpin bends are as steep as 1-in-3 (33%). The ascent holds few terrors for car drivers these days; most problems arise at peak holiday times. And if the road is icy, or you are towing a caravan, don't even consider it!

MILLOM

Sitting on its own peninsula overlooking the estuary of the River Duddon, Millom is well off the beaten track. The town grew with the iron and steel industries in the latter years of the 19th century. The Millom Folk Museum and the Tourist Information Centre are both housed in the imaginatively redeveloped railway station. The museum has vivid reminders of the town's iron-

MUNCASTER CASTLE

mining days, including an impressive full-scale reconstruction of an iron-ore drift mine, as well as items associated with Norman Nicholson, Millom's own poet.

The Hodbarrow Iron Works, which closed in the 1960s, have been encouraged to go back to nature. The result is a brackish lagoon, adjacent to the Duddon Estuary, which is now an RSPB reserve. This stretch of water acts as a magnet for breeding wildfowl, waders and the rare natterjack toad.

MUNCASTER CASTLE

Few stately homes can boast a view to match the panorama from the terrace of Muncaster Castle. Directly below are gardens, featuring one of the largest collection of rhododendrons in the country. In the middle distance the River Esk meanders prettily through the lowlands. The horizon is taken up by a frieze of starkly delineated peaks, of which Scafell Pike at 3,210 feet (978m) is the most prominent.

In 1208 the land at Muncaster was granted to the Pennington family, and is still owned by the family today. The sandstone castle is a major addition to a 14th-century pele tower. Visitors get a guided tour (on audio tape, at least) by the present owner, detailing the many treasures and artworks to be found.

Muncaster Castle is also the headquarters of the World Owl Trust, which is dedicated to worldwide owl conservation. Visitors can see a variety of owls, from the pygmy owl to the gigantic eagle owl, and from native species to some of the rarest owls in the world. On fine summer afternoons visitors get a chance to meet the birds and, weather permitting, watch them in flight.

As Lords of the Manor, the Pennington family owned Muncaster Mill from the 15th century right up to 1961, when the mill closed. The present buildings, dating from about 1700, are easily reached by car on the A595 or by taking a ride on the Ravenglass and Eskdale Railway (the mill is a request halt on the line). The tiny mill, with its overshot wheel turned by water from the River Mite, is a reminder of a time when every village had its own corn mill. Though now restored to working order, the mill is currently closed.

RAVENGLASS

The Roman fort and harbour of Ravenglass were known to the Romans as *Glannoventa*; up to 1,000 men were garrisoned here. Little remains of this settlement, just a short stroll to the south of the village, except for the ruins of the bathhouse. Rising to 12 feet (3.7m), these are probably the highest extant Roman ruins in the country.

Modern-day Ravenglass comprises a short street of attractive houses that ends abruptly at a slipway down to the beach and the estuaries of the rivers Mite and Esk. Inaccessibility to everything but small craft, due to sandbars, meant that Ravenglass never developed its potential as a port.

Ravenglass is well-known the Ravenglass and Eskdale Railway, affectionately known as 'Laal Ratty'. Though it is now one of the most popular attractions in western Lakes, the line has had a distinctly chequered career. The railway (with a 3-foot gauge track) was built in 1875, to carry iron ore (and a few passengers) from the Eskdale mines to the coast and the main Furness line. When the mines became unprofitable, the railway closed.

Operating on a narrower 15-inch gauge track, the line re-opened in 1913 to serve Eskdale's granite quarries and carry a few tourists. Trains plied the narrow-gauge track until they came to a halt once again, in 1953. Fortunately, a group of enthusiasts came to the rescue, helping to buy up the line in 1960, and running it as a tourist attraction. Today the miniature steam locos and carriages operate an extensive service over the seven highly scenic miles (11.2km) between Ravenglass and the terminus at Dalegarth.

WAST WATER

WASDALE & WAST WATER

The bleakly beautiful valley of Wasdale must be approached from the west, and that necessitates a lengthy drive. The reward is that Wasdale will be empty at times when the Lakeland honeypots are teeming.

If the view of the valley seems oddly familiar, that's because the National Park Authority created their logo from this view of Wast Water and the three peaks, Yewbarrow, Great Gable and Lingmell.

Just 3 miles (4.8km) long, Wast Water is the deepest lake in England. Huge screes dominate the southern shore and continue their descent 250 feet (76m) into the water. The road hugs the water's edge until you reach Wasdale Head; communities don't come much smaller or more welcoming than this. The Wasdale Head Hotel is where walkers and climbers congregate to drink beer and swap tales of the mountains. Once you are ensconced in a comfy chair it is easy to forget that you are miles from anywhere.

WAST WATER

ESKDALE & WASDALE

TOURIST INFORMATION CENTRES

Barrow-in-Furness

Forum 28, Duke Street.
Tel: 01229 894784

Millom

Station Buildings. Tel: 01229 774819

PLACES OF INTEREST

Dock Museum

North Road, Barrow-in-Furness.
Tel: 01229 894444

Eskdale Mill

Boot. Tel: 01946 723335

Furness Abbey

Barrow-in-Furness.
Tel: 01229 823420

Hardknott Castle Roman Fort

Western end of Hardknott Pass.

Millom Folk Museum

Station Buildings, Millom.
Tel: 01229 772555
Rooms include a miner's cottage and a blacksmith's forge.

Muncaster Castle, Gardens and Owl Centre

Muncaster. Tel: 01229 717614

Ravenglass and Eskdale Railway

Ravenglass.
Tel: 01229 717171
Steam and diesel trains run along a 7-mile (11.2km) track, through from Ravenglass to Dalegarth.

Ravenglass Roman Bath House

Ravenglass.

FOR CHILDREN

South Lakes Wild Animal Park

Crossgates, Dalton-in-Furness.
Tel: 01229 466086

SHOPPING

Barrow-in-Furness

Market, Wed, Fri & Sat.

Broughton-in-Furness

Market, Tue.

LOCAL SPECIALITIES

Crafts

The *Made in Cumbria* guide to workshops and galleries is available from Tourist Information Centres
www.madeincumbria.co.uk

Cumberland Sausage
Award-winning sausages and hams at Woodall's of Waberthwaite.
Tel: 01229 717237;
www.richardwoodall.co.uk

Cumberland Rum Butter
Available from many local food shops.

Pottery
Gosforth Pottery, near Seascale Gosforth.
Tel: 01946 725296

PERFORMING ARTS

Forum 28 Theatre and Arts Centre
28 Duke Street, Barrow-in-Furness.
Tel: 01229 894489

SPORTS & ACTIVITIES

SEA FISHING

Shoreline around the Isle of Walney and Piel Island. Sea fishing trips can be arranged by Mr S McCoy.
Tel: 01229 826160

BEACH

Silecroft and Haverigg are both award-winning, extensive sandy beaches and are likely to appeal to those look for peace and solitude.

CYCLING

The Eskdale Trail
The Ravenglass and Eskdale Railway provides a virtually traffic-free route in this beautiful valley. Details from stations at Ravenglass or Dalegarth.

Wear to Wear (W2W) Cycle Route
This superb trans-Pennine route (Sustrans Regional Route 20) begins on Walney Island and traverses the southern lakes on its 151-mile (243km) path northeast.

GOLF COURSES

Askam-in-Furness
Dunnerholme Golf Club, Duddon Road.
Tel: 01229 462675

Barrow-in-Furness
Barrow Golf Club,
Rakesmoor Lane, Hawcoat.
Tel: 01229 825444
Furness Golf Club, Central Drive, Isle of Walney.
Tel: 01229 471232

Silecroft
Silecroft Golf Club.
Tel: 01229 774250

GOLF DRIVING RANGE

Barrow-in-Furness

Stroke One Golf Driving and nine-hole course, Hawthwaite Lane, near Roanhead. Tel: 01229 465870

LONG-DISTANCE FOOTPATHS & TRAILS

The Cistercian Way

A 33-mile (52.8km) walk from Grange-over-Sands to Roa Island, near Barrow-in-Furness.

The Cumberland Way

An 82-mile (131.2km) crossing of the Lake District from Ravenglass to Appleby.

The Cumbria Coastal Way

A 124-mile (198.4km) walk from Silverdale to Carlisle.

The Furness Way

A 71-mile (114km) walk from Arnside to Ravenglass crossing the Furness Peninsula.

NATURE RESERVES

Haverigg Nature Reserve, near Millom.

North and South Walney Nature Reserves, Barrow-in-Furness.

Sandscales Haws, Barrow-in-Furness.

RUGBY

Barrow-in-Furness

Barrow Raiders Rugby League Football Club, Craven Park. Tel: 01229 820273

ANNUAL EVENTS & CUSTOMS

Barrow-in-Furness

Barrow Horticultural Society Show, early Sep.

Eskdale

Eskdale Tup (ram) Show, late Sep.

Eskdale Show, late Sep.

Gosforth

Cumbria Riding Club Dressage Show, early Apr.

Gosforth Show, mid-Aug.

Cumbria Riding Club Hunter Trials, early Oct.

Millom

Millom and Broughton Agricultural Show, late Aug.

TEA ROOMS

Fellbites
Dalegarth Station,
Boot, Eskdale
Tel: 01229 717171
www.ravenglass-railway.co.uk
At the valley terminus of 'laal Ratty' the Fellbites café can serve a trainload of passengers at a time with freshly cooked food using local ingredients wherever possible. And you're handy for the train back to Ravenglass!

Broughton Village Bakery
Princes Street, Broughton-in-Furness,
LA20 6HQ
Tel: 01229 716284
Using organic, Fairtrade beans, ground fresh to maximise their flavour, this is a splendid little retreat to enjoy a tall latte or a snappy espresso. You can get a light lunch or snack or try the tempting home-baked cakes.

The Square Café
Annan House, The Square,
Broughton-in-Furness, LA20 6JA
Tel: 01229 716388
www.thesquarecafe.biz
Overlooking the village square, with a few outside tables, this traditional café is popular with walkers, cyclists and motorcyclists. Afternoon teas with home-made scones are a favourite.

Woodlands
Santon Bridge, Nr Holmrook,
CA19 1UY
Tel: 01946 726 281
www.santonbridge.co.uk
With a great view of the local red squirrels, Woodlands is attached to the Santon Bridge Craft Shop and concentrates on home-made food. Very handy for Muncaster Castle and Eskdale as well as Wasdale.

HERDWICK SHEEP

NETHER WASDALE

Boot Inn

Boot, Eskdale CA19 1TG
Tel: 0845 130 6224
www.bootinn.co.uk

Formerly known as the Burnmoor, this friendly pub is good for families. The new conservatory dining area boasts enviable views of the surrounding fells and the garden in the summer.

The Bower House

Eskdale, Holmrook
CA19 1TD
Tel: 01946 723244
www.bowerhouseinn.co.uk

Children will love the outdoor play area. Adults may prefer the real ales and imaginative dishes, which use fresh local ingredients whenever possible. Look out for local Herdwick lamb with minted apple chutney, or the roasted haunch of venison with red wine and juniper berries.

King George IV Inn

Eskdale, Holmrook, CA19 1TS
Tel: 01946 723262
www.kinggeorge-eskdale.co.uk

This 17th-century coaching inn lies in one of Lakeland's finest hidden valleys. Inside you'll find open fires and flagged floors. You can try ostrich fillet or salmon in martini, orange and ginger at this venerable staging post at the junction near Eskdale Green station. Down to earth offerings include pizzas and steak in Old Peculiar pie, with a good range of beers.

Newfield Inn

Seathwaite, Duddon Valley,
Broughton-in-Furness, LA20 6ED
Tel: 01229 716208
www.newfieldinn.co.uk

Deep in the remote Duddon Valley, the Newfield Inn is exactly how you would like to find it – stone floors, real fires, big oak beams. There's a good specials board for food, including pastas and fish, but the local Cumberland sausage is always a favourite.

Western Lakes

BUTTERMERE & CRUMMOCK WATER

COCKERMOUTH

EGREMONT

ENNERDALE

GREAT GABLE

LORTON LOWESWATER

MARYPORT

ST BEES

WHITEHAVEN

INTRODUCTION

The western lakes and shores have features that rival the most beautiful areas, as well as an rich industrial history. Lorton Vale sweeps south from Cockermouth and Buttermere before ending in the lofty Honister Pass. Whitehaven was the third-largest port in Britain, thanks to local industries. Today it has a small fishing fleet, and the harbour has been declared a conservation area. St Bees is also the start of Wainwright's 190-mile (304km) Coast-to-Coast walk to Robin Hood's Bay in Yorkshire. Designated Heritage Coast, part of the cliffs form St Bees Head Nature Reserve.

THACKTHWAITE, LORTON

HOT SPOTS

Unmissable attractions

Explore the area's industrial history of mining coal, slate and iron ore a Maryport...experienced rock climbers can enjoy the thrills of reaching the summit at Napes Needles and fitter walkers can enjoy the delights or Great Gable...experience tranquillity away from the crowds at Ennerdale...explore Whitehaven's harbour, which has been declared a conservation area...enjoy a walk around Loweswater, one of Lakeland's quieter lakes...spectate the World Gurning Championships at Egremont in September...discover the Hay Stacks, near by Buttermere, a modest summit, with dramatic perches, winding trails and magnificent vistas...set off from St Bees to walk part, or all, of Wainwright's Coast-to-Coast walk.

1

1 Buttermere

Surrounded by high hills, the easy, 5-mile (8km), two-hour walk around the edge of Buttermere offers superb views throughout.

2 Ennerdale Water

Ennerdale is 2.5 miles (4km) long and 0.75 miles (1.2km) wide. The water is exceptionally clear and serves West Cumbria as a reservoir. It is the most remote and westerly of the lakes and even in high season offers peaceful tranquillity away from the hordes.

3 Great Gable

W.P. Haskett Smith's remarkable ascent of the south face of Great Gable and Napes Needle, in June 1886 marked the beginning of English rock climbing as a sport. This route to the summit and Napes Needles is only for very experienced rock climbers but there are many gentler routes up Great Gable suitable for fit walkers.

2

3

BUTTERMERE & CRUMMOCK WATER

These two neighbouring lakes in the Buttermere valley, separated only by a half-mile (800m) strip of meadowland, were probably one lake originally. Buttermere is perhaps the more beautiful, although Crummock Water is twice its size and claims to be one of the most impressive waterfalls in the Lakes. Scale Force, on its western side, plunges 172 feet (52m) on its way to the lake.

The path to Scale Force, however, begins in tiny Buttermere village, and is a rough walk to the tree-lined gorge through which Scale Beck plummets. A path leads all the way along Crummock Water's western shore, to join up with the B5289, which runs down the eastern shore. This road links Lorton Vale to the north of Buttermere, with the steep Honister Pass to the east, and continues on to Borrowdale.

Buttermere is also surrounded by high hills, such as the 2,126-foot (648m) Fleetwith Pike which guards the Honister Pass and the 1,959-foot (597m) Hay Stacks. The easy two-hour walk around Buttermere is an impressive one, with superb views in all directions. To the northwest are the Derwent Fells, with Derwent Water beyond, while to the west above Burtness Wood stands a range of dramatic crags and fells.

If you have some time, walk up the road to Buttermere's attractive church, built in 1841, set on a rocky knoll. It is tiny, one of the smallest in the Lakeland area, with a bellcote and a lower chancel. From here there is a lovely view of the valley and the high fells on the south side, all the way to the rocky delights of Hay Stacks, which offers good walking and mild hands-on scrambling.

More than any other fell in the Lakeland, Hay Stacks demonstrates how mere height can often be given an elevation it doesn't deserve. Surrounded by higher fells, this modest summit displays qualities many others lack. It boasts dramatic perches, superb vistas, rocky kolls,

WORDSWORTH'S HOUSE, COCKERMOUTH

LAKE BUTTERMERE

LAKE BUTTERMERE

peat bogs, pretty tarns, even a summit tarn and winding trails. It was rightly described by Alfred Wainwright, as '...a place of great charm and fairyland attractiveness'.

COCKERMOUTH

For a small country market town, Cockermouth has plenty of history behind it. The most significant event as far as most of today's visitors are concerned is that William Wordsworth was born here in 1770. If you first visit modest Dove Cottage in Grasmere, where the poet later lived, the grandeur of his birthplace, a Georgian town house dating from 1745, comes as a surprise. Wordsworth House has been faithfully restored by the National Trust and has been furnished in mid-18th century style, with some of Wordsworth's personal effects.

Other famous names associated with Cockermouth include the mutineer on *The Bounty*, Fletcher Christian, Mary, Queen of Scots and Robert the Bruce.

Insight

EGREMONT CRAB FAIR

The crabs at the Egremont Crab Fair are crab apples not crustaceans. The fair dates from 1267, and on the third Saturday in September the Apple Cart parade passes through the town, and apples are thrown to people lining the route. There are athletics competitions, animal shows, hound trails and a greasy pole competition. In the evening is the event that everyone knows about – the World Gurning Championship. It is more accurately called the 'Gurning through a Braffin' competition, and whoever can make the ugliest grin (gurn) while peering through a horse collar (a braffin), is declared world champion.

CUMBERLAND RUM BUTTER

The name Buttermere comes from the area's rich dairy pastures. Cumberland Rum Butter is a rich concoction which combines local butter with rum, sugar, nutmeg and cinnamon. Traditionally, it was given as a gift to celebrate the birth of a baby, to wish a smooth but spirited life.

ENNERDALE WATER

The town now houses a printing museum, an art gallery at Castlegate House and Jennings' Brewery, which dates from 1828 and offers hour-long guided tours.

EGREMONT

With the River Ehen winding through it, and a wide main street lined with trees (and stalls on its Friday market day), Egremont is a pretty town renowned as the home of ugly faces.

For it is here that the World Gurning Championships are held each September. The country fair in which they take place is almost as old as Egremont Castle, whose ruins stand in a park on a hilltop overlooking the main street. This Norman building of red sandstone dates from the 12th century, though it was largely destroyed in the 16th century; its best surviving feature is the original gatehouse.

Dating from the 16th century is the Lowes Court Gallery on Main Street.The gallery was restored for the promotion of local arts and crafts. Jewellery made from haematite, the local red iron ore, can be bought at the Florence Mine Heritage Centre. This is the last deep working iron-ore mine in Europe, where you will find out why the miners are known as the Red Men of Cumbria. Mining conditions at the turn of the 20th century have been recreated in the Heritage Centre, and a small museum tells the history of the mine.

ENNERDALE

Walkers may appreciate Ennerdale Water more than many other lakes, as access by car is limited and the bulk of its shores can only be explored on foot. Lying in the secluded valley of Ennerdale, its shores are well worth exploring – from the car park at Bowness Knott, a path leads east along the forested northern side of the lake. The land around Ennerdale Water was bought by the Forestry Commission in 1926, and planting began the following year. Behind the rows of spruce and larch, the land rises steeply, to over 2,600 feet (793m) in places. Looking south the hills are higher still, with Pillar at 2,926 feet (892m), in front of which stands Pillar Rock, which has been popular with climbers since its first ascent in 1826.

Ennerdale Water is actually a reservoir serving west Cumbria, and it is possible to walk all the way round, although the going can be tough; the route is 8 miles (12.8km).

GREAT GABLE

There are higher mountains than Great Gable 2,949 feet (899m), but visually it holds its own. If approaching from the southwest from Wast Water and through Wasdale Head, its bulk resembles the great gable end of a house. This imposing approach, which is tough but accessible to fit walkers, is one route up to the top. Another option is from the northeast, from Seathwaite Farm climbing up past the waters of the Sourmilk Gill and passing Great Gable's little brother, Green Gable.

At the top a plaque proudly records the occasion when the surrounding area was given to the National Trust by the Fell and Rock Climbing Club, in memory of their colleagues lost in World War I. A memorial service is held here each year on Remembrance Sunday. It was also in these hills that you can see that modern climbing first started to develop, late in the 19th century. The names alone are inspiring: Needle Ridge, Eagle's Nest Ridge, Windy Gap. The view still inspires, south to Scafell Pike (3,210 feet/978m) and straight down Wasdale towards the Irish Sea.

LORTON

Lorton Vale is the elegant valley that sweeps south from Cockermouth and passes the village of Loweswater, Crummock Water and finally Buttermere before ending in the lofty Honister Pass. Five miles (8km) southeast of Cockermouth is the village of Lorton, which is divided in two. High Lorton clings to the

GREAT GABLE

side of Kirk Fell at the start of the Whinlatter Pass, and is famous for its yew tree.

This magnificent tree which stands behind the village hall (known as Yew Tree Hall, of course) was described by Wordsworth in his poem, 'Yew Trees'. It is further celebrated because it was beneath its boughs that the founder of the Quaker movement, George Fox, preached to a large crowd under the watchful eyes of Cromwell's soldiers. At Whinlatter there is a Forestry Commission Visitor Centre, where you can watch the local ospreys on CCTV and discover more about this vast forest.

LOWESWATER

One of the smaller lakes but is no less delightful for that, Loweswater is often less crowded than those lakes of easier access. To reach it involves a short drive on the B5289 down Lorton Vale from Cockermouth, but many motorists continue down the main road that leads to Crummock Water and Buttermere. Instead, take a turning through Brackenthwaite, which leads along the north shore of the lake with parking at either end. Loweswater village is little more than a church, a village hall and a pub, with a scattering of whitewashed farm buildings surrounded by woodland and meadows. The woods offer many leafy footpaths and are cared for by the National Trust.

MARYPORT

A comparatively new Cumbrian town, it was founded in 1749, Maryport was intended to serve as a port for the coal trade and was named after Mary, the wife of the Lord of the Manor, Humphrey Senhouse II. The port quickly grew, and for a short while was the biggest port in Cumberland, with trade from the coal and iron-ore mines and also a healthy shipbuilding industry.

The story of its rise and subsequent decline is told in the

Maryport Maritime Museum, which also has exhibits ranging from a whale's tooth to telescopes. The museum is in Senhouse Street, which leads to Elizabeth Dock. Also by the quayside is the Lake District Coast Aquarium, which displays a surprising range of native marine and freshwater fish. On the hill above the town, the Senhouse Roman Museum has collections dating from 1570, when John Senhouse rescued some pieces from Maryport's Roman fort. It was added to by the family over the centuries, with some Roman altars, and these are now on show in the Battery, an old naval building overlooking the Promenade and the Solway Firth.

ST BEES

St Bees is the start of Wainwright's famous 190-mile (304km) Coast-to-Coast walk to Robin Hood's Bay in North Yorkshire, not to mention a coast-to-coast cycle route. Popular with walkers, therefore, it is a pleasant village in which to linger before heading off to the east. Before you go inland, take time to explore the impressive sandstone cliffs of St Bees Head, which rise to 462 feet (141m) and which lead to the lighthouse looking over Saltom Bay towards Whitehaven. This part of the coast is Cumbria's only Heritage Coast, with land on the cliffs forming the St Bees Head Nature Reserve. Watch out for puffins, razorbills and kittiwakes, as well as the black guillemot, which breeds nowhere else in England.

In the village itself is the Church of Saint Mary and Saint Bega, which dates back to about AD 650, when it was part of a priory. St Bees also has its own beach, with several other beaches south along the coast. Six miles (9.6km) southeast of St Bees is the Sellafield Nuclear Site and its Visitor Centre, where visitors are treated to a series of displays explaining the Sellafield story and the virtues of nuclear power. Children will enjoy trying to create electricity by pedal power, and

they can even bring home sticks of Sellafield rock for their friends.

WHITEHAVEN

In the middle of the 18th century Whitehaven was the third largest port in Britain, after London and Bristol, thanks to the local industries. Today, Whitehaven has a small fishing fleet, and its harbour is a conservation area, with several monuments to its past mining history, which finally died out in 1986. Your first stop in Whitehaven should be The Beacon, on West Strand, which offers visitors an insight into the history of the town and harbour using audio-visual presentations and exciting displays. On the top floor is the Weather Gallery full of high-tech equipment that monitors and records the weather. On the headland above The Beacon is the winding gear and engine house of the Haig Colliery Mining Museum. Haig was the town's last deep pit, bringing coal from several miles under the sea. Now it records the often tragic stories of the town's mining past, in which more than 1,200 men, women and children died.

The town boasts many handsome Georgian buildings and has two churches that are worth seeking out. St Begh's dates from around 1868 and is visually striking as it was built from white stone with a red stone dressing.

St James' is slightly older, from 1753, with Italian ceiling designs and a very moving Memorial Chapel. It was dedicated first to those who lost their lives in the two World Wars, and later also to local people who were killed in mining accidents. A miner's lamp serves as the Sanctuary lamp.

Book lovers should note that Whitehaven has the largest antiquarian bookshop in Cumbria, and one of the largest in the north. Michael Moon's Antiquarian Bookshop in Roper Street claims to have 100,000 books on its mile (1.6km) of shelving, with room for at least a hundred book browsers.

WHITEHAVEN

WESTERN LAKES

TOURIST INFORMATION CENTRES

Cockermouth
The Town Hall. Tel: 01900 822634

Egremont
Lowes Court Gallery,
12 Main Street. Tel: 01946 820693

Maryport
Town Hall, Senhouse Street.
Tel: 01900 702840

Whitehaven
Market Hall, Market Place.
Tel: 01946 852939

Workington
Carnegie Theatre Foyer, Finkle Street.
Tel: 01900 606699

PLACES OF INTEREST

The Beacon
West Strand, Whitehaven.
Tel: 01946 592302

Castlegate House Gallery
Cockermouth. Tel: 01900 822149

Florence Mine Heritage Centre
Egremont. Tel: 01946 825830

Haig Colliery Mining Museum
Kells, Whitehaven.
Tel: 01946 599949;
www.haig1.freeserve.co.uk

Helena Thompson Museum
Park End Road, Workington.
Tel: 01900 326255

Jennings Brewery
Castle Brewery, Cockermouth.
Tel: 01900 821011

Lake District Coast Aquarium
South Quay, Maryport.
Tel: 01900 817760

Lakeland Sheep and Wool Centre & Cumwest Visitor Centre
Egremont Road, Cockermouth.
Tel: 01900 822673

Lowes Court Gallery
12 Main Street, Egremont.
Tel: 01946 820693

Maryport Maritime Museum
1 Senhouse Street, Maryport.
Tel: 01900 813738

The Printing House
102 Main Street, Cockermouth.
Tel: 01900 824984

The Rum Story
Lowther Street, Whitehaven.
Tel: 01946 592933

Sellafield Visitor Centre
Signposted off A595.
Tel: 01946 727027

Senhouse Roman Museum
The Battery, Sea Brows, Maryport.
Tel: 01900 816168
Wordsworth House
Main Street, Cockermouth.
Tel: 01900 824805

SHOPPING

Egremont
Market, Fri.
Maryport
Market, Fri.
Whitehaven
Market, Thu & Sat.
Michael Moon's Antiquarian Bookshop
19 Lowther Street. Tel: 01946 599010
Workington
Market, Wed & Sat.

LOCAL SPECIALITIES

Beer
Jennings beers.
Cumberland Rum Butter
Available in local shops.

PERFORMING ARTS

Carnegie Theatre and Arts Centre
Workington. Tel: 01900 602122
Civic Hall
Whitehaven. Tel: 01946 852821
Rosehill Theatre
Moresby, Whitehaven.
Tel: 01946 692422

SPORTS & ACTIVITIES

ANGLING

Contact Tourist Information Centres or the National Trust.
Tel: 01539 435599
Loweswater Water End Farm
Tel: 01946 861465

BEACHES

Allonby
Sand and shingle.
Beckfoot
Sand and shingle.
St Bees
Sand and shingle. Fleswick Bay, shingle, sand at low tide.
Silloth
Sand and shingle. Bathing not safe when tide is ebbing.

BOAT HIRE

Loweswater
Water End Farm.
Tel: 01946 861465

WESTERN LAKES

CYCLING

Coast-to-Coast (C2C)
A 140-mile (224km) cycle route linking Whitehaven and Workington to Sunderland.

The Reivers Cycle Route
A 190-mile (306km) route: Tynemouth to Whitehaven.

Hadrian's Cycleway
National Cycle Route 72; a 170-mile (274km) route.

West Cumbria Cycle Network
Routes on disused railways and minor roads.

CYCLE HIRE

Cockermouth
Grinupnorth. Tel: 01900 829600; www.grinupnorth.co.uk

Cleator
Ainfield Cycles, Jacktrees Rd. Tel: 01946 812427

Whitehaven
Haven Cycles, Preston Street. Tel: 01946 63263

Wigton
Wigton Cycle & Sports, 23 West Street. Tel: 01697 342824

GOLF COURSES

Cockermouth
Cockermouth Golf Club, Embleton. Tel: 01768 776223

Maryport
Maryport Golf Club, Bank End. Tel: 01900 812605

St Bees
St Bees Golf Club. Tel: 01946 824300. (9-hole).

Seascale
Seascale Golf Club, The Banks. Tel: 01964 728202

Whitehaven
Whitehaven Golf Club, Red Lonning. Tel: 01946 591144

Workington
Workington Golf Club. Tel: 01900 603460

HORSE-RIDING

Gilcrux
Allonby Riding School. Tel: 01697 322889

Ennerdale
Bradley's, Low Cock How. Tel: 01946 861354

LONG-DISTANCE FOOTPATHS & TRAILS

Coast-to-Coast Walk
A 190-mile (304km) walk from St Bees Head to Robin Hood's Bay.

The West Lakes Way
A 70-mile (112km) walk from Whitehaven to Millom taking in Scafell and Black Combe.

NATURE RESERVES

Contact local TIC or Solway Coast Discovery Centre.
Tel: 01693 33055

SAILING

Crummock Water
Woodhouse, Buttermere.
Permits and boats for hire.
Tel: 01768 770208

Maryport
Maryport Marina.
Tel: 01900 814431

ANNUAL EVENTS & CUSTOMS

Broughton
Children's Carnival, early Jul.

Buttermere
Shepherds' Meet, mid-Sep.
Buttermere Show, early Oct.

Cockermouth
Cockermouth Sheepdog Trials, May.
Cockermouth Carnival, Jun.
Cockermouth Festival, Jul.
Cockermouth and District Agricultural Show, late Jul.

Egremont
West Cumbria Rose Society Show, mid-Jul.
Crab Fair and the World Gurning Championship, Sep.

Ennerdale Bridge
Ennerdale and Kinniside Agricultural Show, late Aug.

Lorton
Vale of Lorton Sheepdog Trials, late Jul.

Loweswater
Loweswater and Brackenthwaite Agricultural Show, mid-Sep.

Maryport
Maryport and District Carnival, early Jul.
Sea Shanty Festival, Aug.

Whitehaven
Copeland Carnival, early Jul.

Workington
Curwen Fair, late May.

TEA ROOMS

Syke Farm

Buttermere, Cockermouth, CA13 9XA

Ice cream is the speciality here, home-made with milk from the farm's resident herd of Ayrshire cattle. But this tiny tea room just below the little church is also great for home-made cakes, bakes and scones, and there's a little craft shop too.

Siskins Café

Whinlatter Forest Visitor Centre, Braithwaite, Keswick, CA12 5TW
Tel: 017687 78410

High up on the Whinlatter Pass, the Forest Visitor Centre and Siskins Café is a great base for exploring the surrounding woodland. From the balcony you can watch the never-ending stream of birds on strategically placed feeders, high in the trees in front of you.

The Gincase

Mawbray Hayrigg, Silloth, Wigton, CA7 4LL
Tel 016973 32020
www.gincase.co.uk

In a converted farm building, where once horses would have powered a grinding stone, the Gincase is a tea room, shop, art gallery and rare breed animal park. On warm days sit in the orchard and enjoy the home-baking in this very quiet spot just a mile or so from the sea.

Harbour Gallery and Café

The Beacon, West Strand, Whitehaven, CA28 7LY
Tel: 01946 592302
www.thebeaconwhitehaven.co.uk

After exploring Whitehaven's historic waterfront, unwind in the peaceful Harbour Gallery Café, surrounded by the artwork of local and community groups. Freshly made sandwiches and snacks are available as well as excellent cream teas. Admission to the adjacent Harbour Gallery is free.

LOWESWATER

Fish Hotel
Buttermere, Cockermouth,
CA13 9XA
Tel: 017687 70253
www.fishhotel.com
Once the home of Mary Robinson, the legendary Maid of Buttermere, the staff at the Fish Hotel pride themselves on understanding the needs of walkers, mountain climbers and fishermen. Beers include Hesket Newmarket's famous ales and tasty bar snacks are also available.

Bridge Hotel
Buttermere, Cockermouth
CA13 9UZ
Tel: 017687 70252
www.bridge-hotel.com
Buttermere's other hostelry is a former 18th-century coaching in and has a lovely garden overlooking Mill Beck. The bar menu includes a good selection of vegetarian options and salads as well as dishes such as Cumberland sausage and Cumberland hotpot. Beers include Theakston's Old Peculiar and Black Sheep Best.

Shepherd's Arms
Ennerdale Bridge,
Cleator, CA23 8AR
Tel: 01946 861249
www.shepherdsarmshotel.co.uk
Located right in the centre of Ennerdale Bridge village this relaxed and informal free house serves Jennings' and Yates's beers. They do a very good line in vegetarian dishes, as well as some tasty creations using fish and locally sourced game, while the two open fires in autumn and winter make it very cosy. Local musicians sometimes play in the bar and the pub is a popular stopping point for weary walkers on the Alfred Wainwright Coast to Coast footpath.

Bassenthwaite & Borrowdale

BASSENTHWAITE LAKE

BORROWDALE

DERWENT WATER

KESWICK

NEWLANDS

SKIDDAW

THIRLMERE

INTRODUCTION

Keswick is at the heart of the northern half of the Lake District. To the south are the wooded surrounds of Derwent Water, which lead to a narrow pass of volcanic rock, the Jaws of Borrowdale. To the north is the great hulk of Skiddaw, built up on softer, smoother slate. To the north are the Scottish mountains and in the far west the Isle of Man. The peaks of the Pennines rise towards the east, while all around are the Lakeland's other hills and dales. Derwent Water attractively dotted with islands, can be explored by one of the ferries that ply the stretches between the seven landing stages around the lake.

DERWENT WATER

HOT SPOTS

Unmissable attractions

Climb Skiddaw, from the top the views are marvellous...experience the atmospheric setting of Castlerigg Stone Circle...gaze upon Derwent Water... discover the industrial remains of a mining community that lived and worked in Newlands Vale...walk through the glorious valley of Borrowdale...stay at Keswick and, if you're feeling fit, climb Skiddaw...take a cruise on Derwent Water and discover marvellous walks, waterfalls and remote islands.

1 Castlerigg Stone Circle
Dating from the early Bronze Age, Castlerigg is one of the most imposing and probably one of the most spectacularly sited ancient monuments in Britain.

2 Derwent Water
Typical of everything that is beautiful in the Lake District, this atmospheric broad lake is ringed by mountain peaks and dotted with mysterious tree-clad islands.

3 Keswick & Skiddaw
If you're staying in Keswick, then Skiddaw is the peak to climb. The Scottish hills, the Isle of Man and the Pennine peaks can be seen from the top of Skiddaw.

4 Newlands Vale
This area was once a busy and thriving mining community. Remnants of the old, aptly named, Goldscope mine can be seen nestling among the bracken of Scope End.

4

SKIDDAW

BASSENTHWAITE LAKE

Owned by the National Park, only quiet activities are permitted on the lake. It is important as a home for a rare fish, the Vendace, as well as for wintering wildfowl, and is designated as a Site of Special Scientific Interest and a National Nature Reserve.

Bassenthwaite village is to the northeast, a short distance from the lake. Near the village, Trotters World of Animals is good for children.

Beside the A591 are the grounds of 17th-century Mirehouse, which lead down to the eastern shores of the lake and incorporate adventure playgrounds and a tea room set in the former sawmill. Nearby is the Norman Church of St Bega. It is an inspiring setting, with Skiddaw (3,054 feet/931m) rising in the east. The location by the lake certainly inspired Tennyson, a regular visitor, who described, in *Morte d'Arthur*, the dying King Arthur being carried across the waters of the lake on a barge, thus making Bassenthwaite Lake the last resting place of

ST BEGA'S CHURCH

Excalibur. A waymarked walk in the grounds allows visitors to enjoy the lakeside scenery, and to watch for a sword rising out of the water!

Mirehouse has been owned by the same family since 1688. It has a wild-flower meadow and a walled garden, while inside is a collection of furniture, portraits and manuscripts reflecting family friendships with Tennyson, Wordsworth, Francis Bacon, Thomas Carlyle and Edward Fitzgerald, respected English poet and translator of *The Rubáiyát of Omar Khayyám*.

BORROWDALE

This glorious wooded valley, which runs south from Derwent Water, contains two of the Lake District's most dramatic natural features – the Bowder Stone and the Jaws of Borrowdale. The Stone is signposted along a path east of the B5289 Borrowdale road, south of the village of Grange. Why stop to look at a stone? Well this one weighs about 2,000 tons and appears to be balanced, ready to topple over. A set of steps leads up to the top of its 36 feet (11m), and despite the attempts of almost everyone who visits to give it a push, it hasn't fallen yet. It was put into place by a glacier, which later melted around it.

Visit

CASTLERIGG STONE CIRCLE

Just 2 miles (3.2km) east of Keswick is one of the most dramatic and atmospheric stone circles in Britain. It dates from about 2,000 BC, but its purpose is unknown, adding to its enigmatic qualities. The 38 stones in the circle itself, with a further 10 set in the centre, are surrounded by high fells, with Helvellyn to the southeast. They are made of volcanic Borrowdale rock, brought here by the glaciers of the Ice Age. The construction is actually oval in shape, 107 feet (33m) across at its widest point, and the name means 'the fort on the ridge', though no evidence of any fort exists here. Castlerigg Stone Circle is in the expert hands of the National Trust.

CASTLERIGG STONE CIRCLE

Here, too, are the so-called Jaws of Borrowdale, where the high crags on either side of the valley almost meet, squeezing the road and the river (the B5289 and the River Derwent) together as they both try to get through. Both do, and the road then swings round to the west, through the village of Seatoller, to climb through the equally dramatic Honister Pass, which links Borrowdale with Buttermere.

DERWENT WATER

South from Keswick spreads Derwent Water, it is the lakeland's widest lake at 1.25 miles (2km) and is attractively dotted with islands. These include, in the very centre, St Herbert's Island, named for the saint who lived here as a hermit in the 7th century. Derwent Isle was once home to German miners who came to work around Keswick and the Newlands Valley in the 16th century. With Borrowdale closing in to the south, and crags on either side of the lake's southern half, Derwent Water is a popular favourite. Popular too is the way in which it can be explored by using the ferries which run between the seven landing stages around the lake, allowing visitors to get off and walk the many footpaths through the surrounding woods and up to the various viewpoints. There are also good views from the high narrow road on the lake's western edge.

The eastern side is rich in waterfalls, such as the spectacular Lodore Falls in the southeastern corner, which is one of the stops for the ferries. Much of the land here is owned by the National Trust. This is largely due to the efforts of Canon Hardwicke Rawnsley, vicar of Crosthwaite, the parish church of Keswick. He was Secretary of the National Trust from its formation until his death in 1920. The beautiful Friar's Crag, on the northern shore of Derwent Water close to the Keswick boat landings, was given to the National Trust (along with Lords Island and Calf Close Bay) to be his

DERWENT WATER

20 TO CARRY 3

DERWENT WATER

memorial. The view from here was deemed by Ruskin 'to be one of the finest in Europe'.

KESWICK

Keswick is a natural centre for mountain climbers, country walkers and more leisurely tourists alike. It is small, with a population of under 5,000, but is said, for its size, to have more beds for guests than anywhere else in the country. This gives an idea of what it can be like on a sunny bank holiday weekend.

If now reliant on tourism, in the past it was mining that kept it alive. The industry flourished in the 16th century with the formation, at the behest of Elizabeth I, of the Company of Mines Royal. Expert miners came from Germany and settled on Derwent Isle. But as the mining industry declined by the second half of the 19th century, so a new source of prosperity came in 1865 when the Cockermouth–Penrith railway line was built, bringing mass tourism and prosperity to the area.

Graphite is the reason the Cumberland Pencil Museum exists here today. A delightfully quirky collection, it shows that even the humble pencil has a fascinating history. The first was made locally in the 1550s, though you can see modern production methods too, and the largest pencil in the world!

Even if you are not mad on cars, you'll find that the Cars of the Stars Motor Museum is a fascinating collection. The museum, includes a Fiat from 1972 painted to look like the Noddy Car. The 'Star Cars' range from one of the Robin Reliants used in *Only Fools and Horses*, to a Morris 8 Tourer driven by James Herriot in *All Creatures Great and Small*, and a selection of glamourous cars used in the James Bond films, including several Aston Martins.

One of the oldest museums in the county is the Keswick Museum and Art Gallery, which has a good display on Lakeland's literary connections. This covers in particular the poet Robert Southey,

KESWICK AND SKIDDAW

CUMBERLAND PENCIL MUSEUM

who moved to Greta Hall in Keswick (now part of a school) to join his brother-in-law, Coleridge, and remained there for over 40 years until his death in 1843. He became Poet Laureate in 1813. There is also a fine period scale model of the Lake District as it was in the early 19th century and, even older, a 500-year-old mummified cat! The geology collection is of national importance and contains mineral examples from the Caldbeck Fells. Geology is also the key to the Keswick Mining Museum. As well as important mineral collections, there is an excellent bookshop for those interested in industrial archaeology.

On the northern edge of Keswick at Crosthwaite is the Church of St Kentigern, whose best-known incumbant, Canon Rawnsley, was the first Secretary of the National Trust. A friend of Beatrix Potter, he was also an author, journalist, educationalist and orator. His influence pervades almost every corner of Keswick and Cumbria.

Insight

BEAR POET

Robert Southey (1774–1843) is perhaps the least known today of the Lakeland poets, despite the fact that he was Poet Laureate for 30 years. One of his works, however, has become such a well-known story that it is often believed to be a traditional fairy-tale. Not so. Robert Southey wrote the original story of *The Three Bears*, although the character of Goldilocks was a later anonymous embellishment.

NEWLANDS

In the delightful Newlands valley, with its rolling green fields, there is little evidence left today that this was once a busy industrial mining community. In fact you have to search hard to find any communities at all, as there are only a handful of farms and the two tiny hamlets of Little Town and Stair. Having found them, each will stake its own claim to fame. A farmhouse at Stair has the inscription 'TF 1647'.

Insight

ONLY HALF WAY UP

Charles Brown, friend and biographer of the English Romantic poet John Keats, accompanied him in 1818 on a walking tour through northern England, Scotland and Ireland. In his journal Brown wrote of their climb up Skiddaw from Keswick, and this extract shows that walking up mountains is the same for everyone:

'A promising morning authorised a guide to call us up at four o'clock, in order to ascend Skiddaw. The distance to the summit from the town is a little more than six miles (9.6km). Its height, from the level of the sea, is 3,022 feet (922m); but only 1,952 feet (595m) above Derwent Water – so lofty is all this part of the country. Helvellyn and Skawfell are somewhat higher, but the view from Skiddaw is esteemed the best. In a short time the continued steep became fatiguing; and then, while looking upward to what I thought was no very great distance from the top, it sounded like cruelty to hear from our guide that we were exactly half way!'

The initials are believed to be those of Thomas Fairfax, commander of the Parliamentary forces, who stayed here during the turmoil following the end of the Civil War in 1646. Little Town's fame could hardly be more different, as its name features in Beatrix Potter's, *The Tale of Mrs Tiggywinkle*.

Copper and lead were mined on the valley's eastern slopes, and small deposits of silver and gold were also found there. Today the landscape has returned to nature, a beautiful, gentle and green landscape down in the valley, but rising up through a steep and rugged pass in the southwest before descending to Buttermere.

SKIDDAW

When the Lakes first began to attract tourists in numbers in the 19th century, it was to Keswick that many of them came, and the one peak they would all walk to was Skiddaw. It is not the most attractive ascent lower down, but even though

NEWLANDS VALE

SKIDDAW

it rises to 3,054 feet (931m) it is a safe and manageable climb of a little more than two hours. You can even avoid the first 1,000 feet (305m) by parking at grid reference NY281254 above the village of Applethwaite, north of Keswick off the A591, and start the climb there. In both places the path to Skiddaw is clearly signed. At peak times walkers will be going up in droves, so this isn't a walk for those seeking solitude.

The rewards are at the top, however, even if you do have to share them. To the north are the Scottish mountains, and in the far west is the Isle of Man. The Pennine peaks rise towards the east, while all around are Lakeland's other hills and dales. If you want to escape the crowds then take the Cumbria Way, which circles behind the main peak into the area known as 'Back o' Skiddaw'.

THIRLMERE

The A591 runs along the eastern side of the long thin lake of Thirlmere, with a car park near Wythburn chapel, built in the 17th century, at the southern end. From here a track leads up to Helvellyn, and before 1879 many a path would have led downwards, too. For the chapel is all that remains of Wythburn village, flooded in the 19th century when Thirlmere was dammed at the northern end and turned into Manchester's first Lakeland reservoir. Armboth in the northwest is also now beneath the waters, along with several farms on the shores of the original lake.

Thirlmere, an attractive, tree-fringed expanse, is one of the few lakes that can be driven, as well as walked, around. A minor road runs down the western edge, a lovely drive through the lakeside woods with several car parks, each with forest trails leading off from them. One trail leads north up to Raven Crag, and there are good views are also to be had halfway down the western edge at Hause Point, where the lake was once narrow enough to have had a bridge.

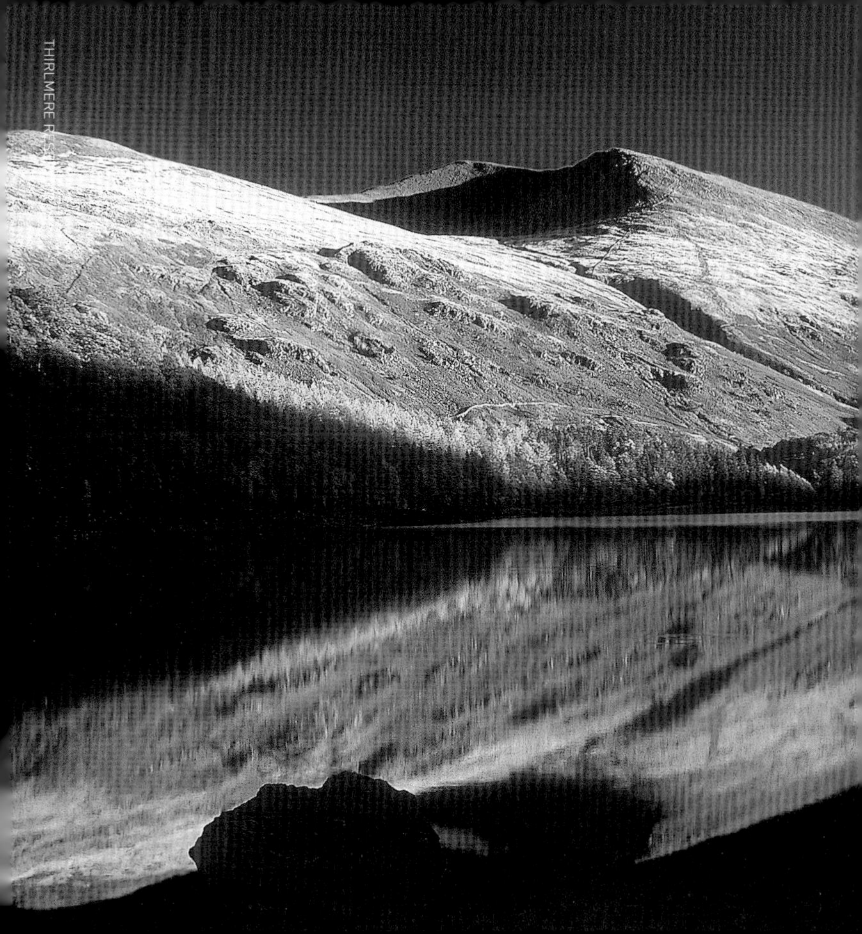

THIRLMERE

INFORMATION

TOURIST INFORMATION CENTRES

Keswick
Moot Hall, Market Square.
Tel: 01768 772645

Silloth
Solway Coast Discovery Centre, Liddle Street.
Tel: 01697 331944

PLACES OF INTEREST

Cars of the Stars Motor Museum
Standish Street, Keswick.
Tel: 01768 773757. Vehicles from television and film.

Castlerigg Stone Circle
2 miles (3.2km) east of Keswick.

Cumberland Pencil Museum
Southey Works, Carding Mill Lane, Keswick.
Tel: 01768 773626
Displays of the history of the pencil and details of modern production methods.

Honister Slate Mine
Honister Pass.
Tel: 01768 777230
Working mine underground tours.

Keswick Mining Museum
Otley Road. Tel: 017687 80055
Mining memorabilia and an exceptional bookshop devoted to geology and industrial archaeology.

Keswick Museum and Art Gallery
Fitz Park, Station Road, Keswick.
Tel: 01768 773263
Displays of letters and manuscripts; also local geology and natural history.

Threlkeld Quarry and Mining Museum
Threlkeld, near Keswick.
Tel: 01768 779747
Exhibits in a former quarry illustrate all aspects of Cumbrian mining, quarrying and geology.

Mirehouse
3 miles (4.6km) north of Keswick, off the A591.
Tel: 01786 772287
Seventeenth-century house where Tennyson wrote 'Morte d'Arthur'. Walled garden, lakeside walks, four adventure playgrounds.

Solway Coast Discovery Centre
Liddle Street, Silloth.
Tel: 01697 333055
www.solwaycoastaonb.org.uk
Interpreting 10,000 years of the Solway's history.

Whinlatter Forest Visitor Centre
Whinlatter Forest Park, near Keswick.
Tel: 01768 778469
Viewing points for local ospreys and other birds as well as interactive displays, walking and cycling trails and an adventure play area.

FOR CHILDREN

Trotters World of Animals
Coalbeck Farm, Bassenthwaite, Keswick. Tel: 01768 776239; www.trottersworld.com.
A conservation-oriented zoo, with feeding displays and a soft play area.

SHOPPING

Keswick
Market, Sat.

Silloth
Market, Thu & Sat.

LOCAL SPECIALITIES

Silloth Shrimps
Available from local fishmongers.

Solway Firth Salmon
Available from local fishmongers.

Sweet Cumberland Ham
Available from local butchers.

PERFORMING ARTS

Theatre by the Lake
Lakeside, Keswick.
Tel: 01768 774411

SPORTS & ACTIVITIES

ANGLING

Bassenthwaite Lake
Permits from Keswick TIC or Pheasant Inn.
Tel: 01768 776234

Derwent Water
Permits from Keswick TIC
Watendlath Tarn and Seathwaite Trout Farm.
Tel 01768 777293

BOAT HIRE

Derwent Water

Derwent Water Marina, Portinscale.
Tel: 01768 772912

Keswick Launch.
Tel: 01768 772263

Nichol End Marine, Portinscale.
Tel: 01768 773082

BOAT TRIPS

Derwent Water

Regular passenger service.
Keswick Launch. Tel: 01768 772263

CYCLE HIRE

Keswick

Keswick Motor Co, Lake Road.
Tel: 01768 772064

Keswick Mountain Bike Centre,
Southey Hill Estate. Tel: 01768 775202

GOLF COURSES

Aspatria

Brayton Park Golf Club, Brayton Park.
Tel: 01697 320840

Keswick

Keswick Golf Club, Threlkeld Hall.
Tel: 01768 779324

Silloth

Silloth-on-Solway Golf Club,
The Clubhouse.
Tel: 01697 331304

HORSE-RIDING

Silloth

Stanwix Park Holiday Centre.
Tel: 01697 332861

Troutbeck, Penrith

Rookin House Farm.
Tel: 01768 483561

LONG-DISTANCE FOOTPATHS & TRAILS

The Allerdale Ramble

A 55-mile (88km) walk from the Borrowdale valley to Silloth.

The Cumbria Coastal Way

A 124-mile (198.4km) walk from Milnthorpe to Carlisle.

SAILING

Bassenthwaite

Bassenthwaite Sailing Club.
Tel: 01768 776341

Derwent Water

Derwent Water Marina.
Tel: 01768 772912
Platty Plus, Lodore Boat Landing.
Tel: 01768 776572
Nichol End Marine. Tel: 01768 7 73082

WATERSPORTS

Derwent Water

Derwent Water Marina, Portinscale.
Tel: 01768 772912. Canoeing and windsurfing.
Nichol End Marine. Tel: 01768 773082
Platty Plus, Lodore Boat Landing.
Canoeing and windsurfing are available. Tel: 01768 776572

ANNUAL EVENTS & CUSTOMS

Bassenthwaite

Sailing Week, early Aug.

Borrowdale

Borrowdale Shepherds' Meet and Show, mid-Sep.

Caldbeck

Caldbeck and Hesket Newmarket Sheepdog Trials, late Aug.
Hesket Newmarket Show, early Sep.

Keswick

Keswick Literature Festival, Mar.
Keswick Jazz Festival, mid-May.
Keswick Mountain Festival, May.
Carnival, mid-Jun.
Keswick Convention, mid to late Jul.
Keswick Victorian Fair, early Dec.

Silloth

Kite Festival, mid-Jul.
Silloth Carnival, August Bank Holiday.
Trawler Race, early Aug.
Solfest, late Aug.

Threlkeld

Threlkeld Sheepdog Trials, mid-Aug.

Uldale

Uldale Village Show, early Sep.
Uldale Shepherds' Meet and Blencathra Hunt, early Dec.

TEA ROOMS

The Watermill Café

Priest's Mill, Caldbeck, CA7 8DR
Tel: 016974 78369
www.watermillcafe.co.uk

Overlooking the River Caldew, this beautifully restored monastic mill site houses craft shops as well as the Watermill Café. Fairtrade and vegetarian options are a speciality and on warmer days you can sit on the terrace, which also overlooks the village cricket pitch.

Flock In

Yew Tree Farm, Rosthwaite, Borrowdale, CA12 5XB
Tel: 017687 77675

On a working fell farm in Borrowdale, it's no surprise that the local Herdwick lamb crops up in many of the snacks on offer here. Royal patronage may have helped raise the profile of this diversification project, but the fruit-studded tea bread and buttery shortbread are seriously tasty too.

Grange Bridge Cottage Tea Shop

Grange in Borrowdale, Borrowdale, CA12 5UQ
Tel: 017687 77201

Just a few yards from the famous double bridges, this 400-year-old cottage is home to a favourite on the Borrowdale teashop trail. Home-baked cakes, cream teas and light lunches are served in the beautiful Riverside Tea Garden.

Seathwaite Farm

Seathwaite, Borrowdale, CA12 5XJ
Tel: 017687 77293

A simple hill-walkers' tea stop, this is the end of the road for motorists and the wettest place in England. But there are home-made scones and flapjacks to be had and on dry days you can sit outside and soak up the serene mountain atmosphere.

ROSTHWAITE

DERWENT WATER

Coledale Inn
Braithwaite, Keswick, CA12 5TN
Tel: 017687 78272
www.coledale-inn.co.uk
A large building that has in turn been a woollen mill and a pencil factory. Now it houses a popular walkers' pub. Fresh fish is a feature of the menu, backed up by beef and lamb dishes and a good selection of local ales.

The Old Crown
Hesket Newmarket, CA7 8JD
Tel: 01697 478288
www.theoldcrownpub.co.uk
A beacon in many respects, despite its slightly dilapidated exterior, the Crown is considered to be at the cutting edge of modern country pubs. This may be because it is co-operatively owned by the locals, or because the little brewery at the back produces some of Cumbria's finest ales, or may be that the crack is unfailingly excellent.

King's Head
Thirlspot, Keswick, CA12 4TN
Tel: 017687 72393
www.lakedistrictinns.co.uk
This old coaching inn is surrounded by hill scenery. Inside there is a wide choice of regional beers and a menu that makes extensive use of local ingredients and recipes – Cumberland sausage from Waberthwait, duck confit or Jennings steak and ale pie.

The Swinside Inn
Newlands Valley, Keswick, CA12 5UE
Tel: 017687 78253
www.theswinsideinn.com
Sitting on the far side of Swinside, this old inn has great views of both Causey Pike and Catbells. Fresh local ingredients include Borrowdale trout and Swinside chicken. Beers tend to be Scottish and Jennings.

ULLSWATER

Ullswater, Penrith & Eastern Fells

APPLEBY-IN-WESTMORLAND

HAWESWATER

HELVELLYN

HUTTON-IN-THE-FOREST

PENRITH

SHAP & KELD

TEMPLE SOWERBY

ULLSWATER

INTRODUCTION

This is a very varied corner of the Lake District. To the south and west is what you would expect from the area: large expanses of water, such as Haweswater and Ullswater, surrounded by soaring mountains like Helvellyn. Head further east, however, and you move through the rolling green Eden Valley, beyond which stand the rugged Pennine hills. There are market towns and ancient monuments, border towns and castles, stately homes and gardens – and fewer crowds.

SHAP ABBEY

HOT SPOTS

Unmissable Attractions

Head up to Penrith Beacon on Penrith Hill, which used to be lit to warn the inhabitants that border reivers (robbers) raids were imminent but today makes a fine viewpoint...head west to Ullswater and the Aira Force waterfall, where William Wordsworth and his sister spied the 'daffodils so beautiful'...visit the southern tip of the lake below the shoulders of Helvellyn via Kirkstone Pass, Wordworth's favourite mountain and the favourite of countless thousands, who trek to its summit – it's a grand climb...enjoy the abundant wildlife in the Haweswater Valley with peregrine falcons, buzzards, sparrowhawks and even golden eagles now breeding in the valley.

1 Ullswater
Undoubtedly one of the area's loveliest lakes, its waters are exceptionally clear and are surrounded by soaring mountains including Helvellyn, Wordsworth's favourite.

2 Appleby Castle
In the heart of the Eden Valley lies the grand Appleby Castle, surrounded by 25 acres (10ha) of parkland. Inside the Great Hall there are collections fine paintings and furnishings.

3 Penrith Castle

Visitors access the striking medieval sandstone remains via a wooden footbridge that spans the castle's moat.

4 Aira Force

Climb the tree-clad gorge of Aira Beck to pass two waterfalls. The lower, larger and more famous waterfall is Aira Force. The Upper falls are High Force and are also very impressive, particularly when in spate. Broader than Aira Force, the upper falls, resemble the rapids of an American river canyon.

4

APPLEBY CASTLE

APPLEBY-IN-WESTMORLAND

Appleby has a great deal to commend it, including its setting, in a loop of the tree-lined River Eden, above which its Norman castle stands protectively. Appleby Castle has an impressive 11th-century keep, although a lot of the building dates from the 17th century when it was restored by the redoubtable Lady Anne Clifford. Unfortunately the castle is currently closed to visitors.

Appleby was once the county town of Westmorland, with a royal charter dating from 1174. At either end of its main street, Boroughgate, the High Cross and the Low Cross mark what were the boundaries of Appleby market. The attractive almshouses, known as Lady Anne's Hospital, are still maintained by a trust fund set up by Lady Anne Clifford to provide accomodation for 13 widows. Lady Anne is buried here in Appleby, her tomb lying in St Lawrence's Church, which can also boast one of the oldest surviving working church organs in England.

The attractive village of Morland, which is situated 7 miles (11.2km) northwest of Appleby, has won several Best Kept Village awards, and the village church has an Anglo-Saxon tower, the oldest in Cumbria.

HAWESWATER

It may sound like another of nature's lakes, but modern Haweswater is in fact a reservoir, created in the 1930s. Beneath its surface lies the village of Mardale Green and dairy farms of the Haweswater valley.

However, wildlife abounds in the area, with peregrine falcons, buzzards, sparrowhawks and even golden eagles now breeding in the valley. The eagles are closely monitored by the RSPB, but an observation post allows visitors to watch their activities from a distance. Otters have also colonised the area, no doubt feeding on the rare char and freshwater herring that are also found here. Other mammals include both roe and red deer, and red squirrels.

On the western shores of the reservoir steep crags rise to Bampton Common, while in the east is the ancient Naddle Forest, refuge of wood warblers, tree pipits, redstarts and several species of woodpeckers. The path which winds through the woods is part of a circular walk around Haweswater and one of the best circular walks in the Lake District.

HELVELLYN

Wordsworth's favourite mountain is the favourite of thousands more, who regularly trek to its summit at

Visit

NENTHEAD

Nenthead Mines Heritage Centre tells the story of how the Quaker London Lead Company left a remarkable social and economic legacy in the north Pennines. The centre, the mines and the village evoke a vivid reminder of past life and industry in this remote upland landscape.

HAWESWATER

HELVELLYN

3,116 feet (949m). It is indeed a grand climb, but its popularity should not mask its difficulty, as it has arduous stretches, especially on its jagged eastern edges. If you're thinking of venturing on to the hill, make sure you're prepared for sudden changes in weather. Snowfall is not unknown on the tops even as late as June, and dense mist can envelop them at any time. If you're a novice, try joining one of the many organised groups.

Warnings aside, the peak is accessible by reasonably fit walkers in possession of the relevant OS map, a popular approach being from Wythburn on the southeastern shores of Thirlmere reservoir. This takes the walker up Helvellyn's steep southwestern slopes, with splendid views across Thirlmere to the west. The eastern approaches are longer but scenically more dramatic, from Grisedale or Glenridding, for example.

The arduous climb may have taken your breath away, but so will the views from the top of Helvellyn, from here you'll be able to enjoy views to the north along the valley towards Keswick, and east beyond the mountain lake, Red Tarn, to the distant high peaks of the Pennines.

Just south of the summit is a memorial by Wordsworth and Sir Walter Scott. The words are a sign that you have reached the highest point in the Lake District. Only Scafell Pike, at 3,210 feet (978m), and Scafell, at 3162 feet (964m), are higher than Helvellyn.

HUTTON-IN-THE-FOREST

Hutton-in-the-Forest, 7 miles (11km) northwest of Penrith, sounds like a tucked-away fairy-tale village. In fact, it has been the stately home of the Vane family since 1600. It was originally owned by the de Huttons family on land they were granted in return for caring for the deer reserve, and for holding the king's stirrup whenever he mounted his horse in Carlisle Castle. Some of the older features include a magnificent 17th-century gallery and grand hall.

Activity

CONSERVING CUMBRIA

Visitors can help the environment by parking their cars and using the waymarked walks, cycling, taking the local trains, buses, minibus tours and launches on the lakes. During the summer an open-top bus service operates between Bowness, Windermere, Ambleside and Grasmere. The Coniston Rambler links Windermere, Ambleside, Hawkshead and Coniston and a service from Keswick leaves for Borrowdale and Buttermere. Minibus tours are a popular way of seeing the high passes; their main centres are Windermere and Keswick.

The grounds are worth seeing, as the present owners take an active interest in their development, yet also allowing parts to remain wild. A particular treat is a walled garden dating from from the 1730s and a wild-flower meadow. There is also a lake where nature is largely allowed to take its own course.

PENRITH

Another borders market town that proved vulnerable to Scottish raiders, Penwith was sacked in the 14th century. Penrith Beacon on Beacon Hill at the town's northern edge was lit to warn the inhabitants of impending raids, and today it is a good viewpoint. The ruined red sandstone castle (English Heritage), which stands in Castle Park, dates from the early 15th century.

There are many more buildings of architectural and historical interest, including Penrith Museum and St Andrew's Church; its graveyard contains the reputed grave of Caesarius, the giant 10th-century Cumbrian king. Sandgate Hall is a 17th-century town house, unaltered since it was built apart from the modern windows. Potter's Lodge, on the corner of Fell Lane and Scaws Drive, is a very fine example of Georgain Architecture

Just 1 mile (1.6km) south of Penrith at Eamont Bridge stands the Mayburgh Earthwork. Dating from

HUTTON-IN-THE-FOREST

NINE STANDARDS, NEAR SHAP

PENRITH CASTLE

prehistoric times, its 15-foot (4.5m) banks surround an area of 1.5 acres (0.6ha), inside which is a huge and solitary stone. Close by King Arthur's Round Table is another ancient henge monument.

Wetheriggs Country Pottery, 4 miles (6.4km) south of Penrith, has been here since 1855 and the steam-powered pottery can still be toured. Several different craftspeople are likely to be working at any one time, and visitors can try their hand at throwing the clay.

Rheged – Upland Kingdom Discovery Centre on the A66, interprets the history of the area through film and a range of innovative techniques. It is also home to the National Mountaineering Exhibition.

SHAP & KELD

Shap stone has been used in the making of many fine monuments but the village's own monument is Shap Abbey, by the River Lowther. It was founded in 1199 by the

Insight

PENRITH BEACON

The last time the beacon was lit was in 1745. In an attempt to restore James Stuart, the 'Old Pretender' to the throne as James III, the Jacobites rose in 1715 and walked south with an army of Highlanders. Joined by the Earl of Derwentwater and 'a parcel of Northcountry jockeys and foxhunters at Brampton', they advanced on Penrith.

The beacons were fired and the Cumberland and Westmorland militia called out. Accompanied by several thousand yeomen, farmers and labourers they marched to intercept the Jacobite forces at Penrith Fell. However, when they encountered the advancing guard, the defending army ran away leaving their commanders, Lord Lonsdale and Bishop Nicholson to fend for themselves. Lonsdale fled to Appleby and the bishop to Rose Castle.

The Jacobites levied a contribution of £500 on Penrith but otherwise left it undistrubed. They did however plunder Lowther Hall.

Premonstratensian Order also known as the White Canons from the colour of their habits. The west tower is the most imposing part of the remains, and dates from about 1500. After the Dissolution of the Monasteries, part of the area here was used as a quarry, but the Abbey remains are now safe in the hands of English Heritage.

The National Trust look after the 15th-century Keld Chapel, in the hamlet of Keld. The simple chapel is still used for occasional services, but is normally locked, though instructions for obtaining the key are pinned to the chapel door.

TEMPLE SOWERBY

For those who want to see and be inspired by a true host of golden daffodils in the Lake District, then you will find one of the finest spring displays is at Acorn Bank Garden, Temple Sowerby. Whole swathes of yellow daffodils bob in the wind beneath the grand oak trees that form an important part of these 2.5 acres (1ha), owned by the National Trust. Acorn Bank is particularly noted for its walled herb garden, which contains the largest collection of medicinal, culinary and even narcotic herbs in the north of England; in all some 250 species. Some are poisonous, so you are warned not to try nibbling them! There are traditional orchards, too, and fine collections of roses, shrubs and herbaceous borders. Gardeners can stock up with a choice of plants from the small shop.

The garden is not just of interest to gardeners though. A circular woodland walk has been created, which makes for a pleasant stroll as it takes the visitor for part of the way through woods alongside Crowdundle Beck and to the restored watermill.

It is the gardens here that originally provided the name for the nearby village of Temple Sowerby, located between Penrith and Appleby. It is known that as long ago as 1228 the Knights Templar

TEMPLE SOWERBY

AIRA FORCE

had a religious house on this spot, however the oldest parts of the present buildings date back to the 16th century. Nor is the herb garden an ancient one, it was started by the National Trust who took over care of the gardens in 1969.

ULLSWATER

On the western shores of Ullswater, a series of splendid waterfalls tumbles down through the wooded gorge of Aira Beck which flows into the region's second largest lake, some 7.5 miles (12km) long. The falls are known by the name of the largest, the 70-foot (21.3m) drop of Aira Force, on land owned by the National Trust. There's also an arboretum, a café and a landscaped Victorian park.

Back in 1802, the falls didn't just feed the waters of Ullswater, they fed the imagination of William and Dorothy Wordsworth. The poet and his sister were walking near by, when Dorothy observed the 'daffodils so beautiful... they tossed and reeled and danced.' Her words were transformed into one of the best-known and best-loved of English poems, William Wordsworth's *Daffodils*. Aira Force itself is also the setting for another of William Wordsworth's poems, *The Somnambulist*.

It is appropriate that the poet was inspired by what, for many people, is the lake among lakes, indisputably beautiful. The southern tip of its slim shape is below the shoulders of Helvellyn, to the west, and is reached through the dramatic and high Kirkstone Pass, which rises to 1,489 feet (454m). Near here is the Kirkstone Pass Inn, third highest pub in the country. Look, too, for the rock which is said to resemble a church steeple and which gives the pass its name – church-stone.

At Pooley Bridge on the lake's northern tip, a fish market used to be held in the main square, and this area is still rich in trout and salmon. A short walk up to Dunmallard Hill reveals Iron Age remains and

lovely views. Below here at the pier near the 16th-century bridge, two 19th-century steamers leave to take visitors down the lake. The two ships, *Lady of the Lake* and *Raven*, date from 1877 and 1889 respectively, an indication of how long visitors have been enjoying these waters.

The steamers call at Howtown, roughly halfway along Ullswater's eastern shore, then travel on to Glenridding at the southern end. A popular option is to combine a cruise with a walk, and no finer walk is said to exist in the Lakes than that between Howtown and Glenridding.

For much of the way the footpath skirts Ullswater's shores, with fine views across the waters and Helvellyn rising beyond. There is no road through this steep-cliffed southeastern shore. The cruise boat can then be rejoined at Glenridding, but don't let the distances deceive you. The lake may be only 7.5 miles (12km) long, but that is also roughly the distance by foot from Howtown to Glenridding. The curve of its crescent shape here accounts for the rest, with an extra stretch round the bottom loop of the lake.

A visit to Glenridding itself is definitely worthy of your time. It has an information centre, inns and a variety of shops and places of interest. It is now the main gateway to the high Helvellyn masif and a popular place for hillwalkers and climbers to congregate. Until the 1960s it was also an important mining village. The Greenside Lead Mine, located at the top of the valley, was the largest lead mine in Britain. All is quiet now, and a youth hostel occupies a former mine building.

Near Howtown the lake narrows to about 400 yards (366m) at the strangely named Skelly Nab. The name derives from the freshwater herring, the schelly, found only here, in Haweswater and high up in the Red Tarn on Helvellyn. The silvery foot-long fish were once caught in nets strung between Skelly Nab and the opposite shore.

POOLEY BRIDGE BOATHOUSE

TOURIST INFORMATION CENTRES

Alston
The Railway Station. Tel: 01434 382244

Appleby-in Westmorland
Moot Hall, Boroughgate.
Tel: 01768 351177

Penrith
Robinson's School, Middlegate.
Tel: 01768 867466

Southwaite
M6 Service Area. Tel: 01697 473445/6

Rheged Discovery Centre
Redhills, Penrith. Tel: 01768 860034

Ullswater
Main Car Park, Glenridding.
Tel: 01768 482414

PLACES OF INTEREST

Acorn Bank Garden
Temple Sowerby.
Tel: 01768 361893
Delightful garden by Crowdundle Beck.

Brougham Castle
Brougham. Tel: 01768 862488

Brougham Hall
Brougham.
Tel: 01768 868184
Craft centre and museum in a 15th-century ruin.

Dalemain
Pooley Bridge, Dacre.
Tel: 01768 486450
Delightful country house with gardens and parkland.

Hutton-in-the-Forest
Skelton. Tel: 01768 484449

Little Salkeld Watermill
Little Salkeld, Penrith.
Tel: 01768 881523

Long Meg Stone Circle
Little Salkeld, Penrith.

Nenthead Mines Heritage Centre
Nenthead, Alston.
Tel: 01434 382037

Penrith Castle
Opposite Penrith railway station.

Penrith Museum
Robinson's School, Penrith.
Tel: 01768 212228

Rheged Discovery Centre
Redhills, Penrith.
Tel: 01768 868000; www.rheged.com
Exhibitions, restaurant, coffee shop and shops.

Shap Abbey
Shap. Premonstratensian abbey moved from Preston Patrick to Shap c1199.

South Tynedale Railway
The Railway Station, Hexham Road, Alston. Tel: 01434 381696

Wetheriggs Country Pottery
Clifton Dykes, Penrith.
Tel: 01768 892733
A steam-powered pottery.

FOR CHILDREN

Eden Ostrich World
Langwathby. Tel: 01768 881771; www.ostrich-world.com
Ostriches and other animals. Indoor soft play area.

Lakeland Bird of Prey Centre
Old Walled Garden, Lowther.
Tel: 01931 712746

SHOPPING

Appleby-in-Westmorland
Open-air market, Sat.

Penrith
Open-air market, Tue. Sat, Sun at Auction Mart.

LOCAL SPECIALITIES

Cumberland Sausage
Butchers, Penrith. Several supply J&J Graham, Market Place, Penrith.

Cheese
Smoked Cumberland cheese and other specialities at Taste@Rheged.

Crafts
Gossipgate Gallery,
The Butts, Alston. Tel: 01434 381806
The Rheged Shop, Rheged Discovery Centre, Redhills, Penrith.
Tel: 01768 868000; www.rheged.com

Mustard
Cumberland mustard is sold in Alston, Taste@Rheged and several other places in the Eden Valley.

Pottery
Wetheriggs Country Pottery, Clifton Dykes, Penrith. Tel: 01768 892733

SPORTS & ACTIVITIES

ANGLING

River Eden, Haweswater & Ullswater

Permits are required. Contact the local TICs, Pickthalls, Mains Farm, Kirkoswald.

Tel: 01768 898342 or Lazonby Parish, c/o Midland Hotel, Lazonby.

Tel: 01768 898901

Blencarn Lake, near Penrith.

Tel: 01768 88284

BOAT TRIPS

Ullswater

Ullswater Navigation and Transit Co. Ltd.

Tel: 01768 482229

CYCLE HIRE

Glenridding

St Patrick's Boat Centre.

Tel: 01768 482393

Penrith

Arragon's Cycle Centre, Brunswick Road.

Tel: 01768 890344

Pooley Bridge

Park Foot Caravan Site.

Tel: 01768 486309

GUIDED WALKS

Appleby-in-Westmorland

Contact the local TIC or East Cumbria Countryside Project.

HORSE-RIDING

Little Salkeld

Bank House Equestrian.

Tel: 01768 881257

Troutbeck, Penrith

Rookin House Farm.

Tel: 01768 483561

LONG-DISTANCE FOOTPATHS & TRAILS

The Pennine Way

The country's premier National Trail traverses the high Pennine ridge between Dufton and Alston.

Coast-to-Coast Walk

A 190-mile (304km) walk from St Bees Head to Robin Hood's Bay, North Yorkshire.

SAILING

Glenridding

Sailing Centre, The Spit.

Tel: 01768 482541

Watermillock

Caravan, Camping and Marine Park.

Tel: 01768 486666

ANNUAL EVENTS & CUSTOMS

Alston

Alston Sheepdog Trials, Jun.
Alston Gala Day, early July.
Alston and District Flower Show, early Sep.
South Tynedale Railway Open Day, early Oct.

Appleby-in-Westmorland

Appleby New Fair (Horse Fair), second week Jun.
Appleby Town Carnival and Sports, mid-Jul.
Jazz Festival, late Jul.
Appleby Agricultural Show, early Aug.
Appleby and District Gardeners' Society Show, early Sep.

Bampton

Bampton Sports Day, Jun.

Lowther

Lowther Horse Driving Trials and Country Fair, early Aug.

Musgrave

Musgrave Rushbearing, Jul.

Patterdale

Patterdale sheepdog trials, end Aug.

Penrith

Fell Pony Stallion Show, May.
Castletown Gala Week, Jun.
Agricultural Show, late Jul.
Potfest, end of Jul.
Lakeland Fell Pony Show, early Aug.

Shap

Shap Sheepdog Trials, Jun.

Skelton

Skelton Show, mid-Aug.

Warcop

Warcop Rushbearing, Jun.

TEA ROOMS

Acorn Bank
Temple Sowerby,
Penrith, CA10 1SP
Tel: 017683 61893
www.nationaltrust.org
A visit to Acorn Bank's tea room is the only chance you'll get to see inside this 17th-century mansion. The National Trust tradition of excellent home-made cakes continues here alongside Fairtrade teas and coffees. Lunches and a children's menu are also available.

Fellbites Café
Glenridding,
Penrith, CA11 0PD
Tel: 017684 82664
At the centre of Glenridding, by the main car parks, Fellbites couldn't be more conveniently placed for visitors to this beautiful valley. Ullswater trout is a favourite on the lunch menu, or you could try one of the many Lakeland-recipe cakes.

The Watermill Tearoom
Little Salkeld,
Penrith, CA10 1NN
Tel: 01768 881523
www.organicmill.co.uk
This little café is attached to the watermill itself. It sells its organic flour and other goodies and has a classroom for various breadmaking courses. The Gallery displays local crafts. After tasting the wholesome vegetarian fare, you can pop next door and watch the flour being milled.

Greystone House Farm Shop and Tearoom
Stainton, Penrith, CA11 0EF
Tel: 01768 866952
The oak-beamed lofthouse tea room is a great place to sample some of the locally sourced ingredients sold in the shop. Lunches, snacks, home-baked scones and cakes are all freshly prepared and a speciality is the farm's own beef and lamb.

DALEMAIN HOUSE

ULLSWATER

GEORGE AND DRAGON

Garrigill, Alston, CA9 3DS
Tel: 01434 381293
www.george-and-dragon-inn.co.uk

Once serving the local lead and zinc mining communities, this 17th-century coaching inn is popular with walkers. Stone-flagged floors and a roaring fire greet visitors to this remote village pub, high in the North Pennines. Excellent for locally produced Cumberland sausage, or a filled Yorkshire pudding. The Black Sheep ales are often accompanied by a guest beer. On a sunny day you can sit outside on the village green.

Horse and Farrier

Dacre, Penrith, CA11 0HL
Tel: 017684 86541

Pub and post office in one, the Horse and Farrier sets the standard for good pubs at the heart of the community. Children are welcome and there are good real ales to wash down the delicious home-baked ham or minted lamb Henry. Vegetarian and salad options are also available.

Traveller's Rest

Greenside Road, Glenridding, Penrith, CA11 0QQ
Tel: 017684 82298

There is no better place to unwind after climbing Helvellyn than in this cosy pub halfway up the road to Greenside mine. Stay for a generous home-cooked meal, or sit outside with a pint and watch the walkers.

The Crown Inn

Kirkoswald, Penrith, CA10 1DQ
Tel: 01768 898435

The more traditional of the two pubs in this village, huddled round its cobbled market square. There's a big open fire, and a quieter snug round the corner from the single bar area. Food has an Italian leaning, but excellent use of local ingredients.

RIVER IRTHING

Carlisle & Borderlands

BEWCASTLE

BIRDOSWALD

BRAMPTON

CARLISLE

HADRIAN'S WALL

INTRODUCTION

This fascinating corner of England is often neglected by guidebooks. Yet Carlisle is only 20 miles (32km) from Keswick for that famous flying crow, if twice the distance in a dog-leg drive. It is a land for those with an interest in its dramatic and often romantic history, for this is a land of reivers, of 'Bonnie' Prince Charlie, of castles and priories, of the Romans and Hadrian's Wall. If its low-lying landscape means less visual drama, there is certainly no lack of the historical kind, with Carlisle's museums, old buildings, castle and cathedral as its focus.

LANERCOST PRIORY

HOT SPOTS

Unmissable attractions

Walk along a section of Hadrian's Wall, 73 miles (117.5km) long and almost 2,000 years old, marking the northern boundary of the Roman Empire...discover Carlisle's rich history at Tuille House Museum and Art Gallery, where you can shoot a crossbow, write on a Roman wax tablet or go down a mine...or walk around the city walls, begun by William Rufus, who recaptured Carlisle from the Scots in 1092...enjoy the peace and quiet at beautiful Lanercost Priory...enjoy the rugged splendour of the border area at Bewcastle...picnic at Birdoswald looking out over the remote remains of the Roman fort and settlement...go shopping at Brampton's market.

1 Lanercost Priory
Set in a serenely beautiful wooded valley near Brampton, Augustinian Lanercost Priory is remarkedly well preserved. It was destroyed in 1296 by Scottish raiders.

2 Hadrian's Wall
Now a World Heritage Site, the Romans' tremendous achievement can still be appreciated; substantial portions of the both the stone wall and the turf ramparts can be seen.

HOT SPOTS

3 Arthuret Church, Longtown
Arthuret Church on the outskirts of Longtown, dates from 1150, but the present Church was built in 1609 in late-Gothic style. Archie Armstrong, favourite Court Jester to James I, and later Charles I, is buried here.

4 Bewcastle Cross
Bewcastle is one of the last, unspoilt areas of Britain and retains all the rugged splendour of the border regions. It is an ideal centre, both to explore, and as a base for visiting the nearby Lake District, Pennines, Cheviots, Scottish Lowlands and Northumberland coast.

5 Carlisle
The award-winning Tullie House Museum and Art Gallery houses in Carlisle combines imaginative displays with a stroll through Roman Carlisle and a climb on part of Hadrian's Wall.

5

BEWCASTLE

In the churchyard of this remote corner of Cumbria, 3 miles (4.8km) east of the B6318 and less than 7 miles (11.2km) from the Scottish border, stands Bewcastle Cross, one of the oldest and finest stone crosses in Europe. It is a cross without its cross, however, as the top fell off and no one knows what happened to it. Still a magnificent sight, however, it stands more than 13 feet (4m) high and is made of yellow sandstone. Its weathered surface is patterned with early Celtic scrolls and intricate designs, and decorated with impressive carvings first made some 1,300 years ago.

Just to the south is Hadrian's Wall, and the ruins of Bewcastle Castle, built in about 1092 on the site of a former Roman fort. The castle's south wall is still standing, to almost its full height, but it is a castle to be appreciated for its setting rather than its state of preservation.

A nearby village pub, the Drove, carries echoes of the one-time drovers' roads, which passed by here. A former inn, near by, was named the Lime Kiln after the lime industry which flourished here. Some old kilns can still be seen in the surrounding countryside, and on the border with Scotland, the remote Bailey district has several limestone quarries well hidden amongst its craggy hills.

BIRDOSWALD

Above the dramatic Irthing Gorge, with a picnic area now looking out over it, the remote 5-acre (2ha) remains of the Roman fort and settlement at Birdoswald is the most interesting spot in this western expanse of Hadrian's Wall. It was built in about AD 125 when its Roman name was *Banna*, and at its busiest would have housed up to 500 foot soldiers. They were there to protect this length of wall, and in particular their bridge across the River Irthing, from the Scots. Although the Wall itself is lower here than it is further east, the part of it which

Visit

TURF WORK

From Harrow's Scar near Birdoswald to its end at the Solway Firth, a distance of 30 miles (48km), Hadrian's Wall was originally made of turf. Its rebuilding in stone took place partly during Hadrian's reign, and partly from AD 160. A 2-mile (3.2km) stretch of the wall west of the River Irthing did not follow the line of the original wall, so some of the remains of the turf wall can still be seen running nearby. Some of the turrets are free-standing, to enable turf ramparts to be run up them.

runs eastwards from Birdoswald towards Harrow's Scar is the longest visible remaining stretch – a strong reminder of its original scale.

Of the fort itself, mainly the perimeter wall remains, with its entrance gates and part of one turret. Nevertheless, with the help of an interactive visitor centre, a vivid picture emerges of Birdoswald in Roman times. Excavations have unearthed the granaries, added in about AD 200, and other finds have included an 'Arm Purse' containing 28 silver coins, and some delicate gold jewellery now on display in Carlisle's Tullie House Museum. A visit here is certainly recommended after seeing the site itself.

BRAMPTON

One of Cumbria's many small and attractive market towns, Brampton has held its charter since 1252. The cobbled square around the Moot Hall bustles each Wednesday, although not as much as it would have done in 1745 when Brampton was the headquarters of Bonnie Prince Charlie's army while it was laying siege to Carlisle Castle. Worth seeking out is St Martin's Church, which has stained-glass windows by William Morris and Burne-Jones.

The Augustinian Priory at Lanercost, in a wooded valley 2 miles (3.2km) northeast of Brampton, was dedicated to St Mary Magdalene in 1169. Although much of it is in ruins,

BIRDOSWALD

CARLISLE CASTLE

including the main priory buildings, the nave of the church still survives and has been used as the parish church from the mid-1700s to the present day. Its vaulted ceilings are splendid. Unfortunately its location, close to the Scottish border, made it the subject of Scottish raids over the centuries, hastening its downfall.

CARLISLE

If you want to begin with the history of Carlisle, then a visit to the award-winning Tullie House Museum and Art Gallery in Castle Street with its interactive displays, is an excellent place to start. It traces the rich history of Carlisle from before the Romans to the railways and beyond, via the reivers, Robert the Bruce and the Roundheads. It also has an excellent range of natural history displays. A great deal of thought has gone into the exhibits, which combine education and entertainment. You can try writing on Roman wax tablets, shoot a crossbow, or go down a mine tunnel.

Insight

WILLIAM WALLACE

William 'Braveheart' Wallace, who is known to have raided Lanercost Priory, was born in about the year 1274. He was an early campaigner for Scottish independence. In 1297 he killed the English sheriff in Lanark, and went on to defeat Edward I's army at Stirling Bridge before moving into northern England. By 1298, however, Edward I's troops had begun to fight back and defeated Wallace at Falkirk. After escaping to France he returned to Scotland but was arrested in 1305. That same year he was hanged, drawn and quartered in London, the quarters of his body were sent to Newcastle, Berwick, Stirling and Perth.

CURIOUS CARLISLE

Carlisle is, by area, the largest city in England and, in Cold Fell, at 2,041 feet (622m), has the highest point in any English city. Thanks to Mary, Queen of Scots, it claims the first international football match and this is where England's first pillar box stood.

Linked to the museum by the Millennium Gallery, Carlisle Castle dates from 1092 when the first castle was built by William II. The keep dates from then, but many of the distinctive rounded battlements were added by Henry VIII to house artillery. Several rooms in the gatehouse are decorated in medieval style, while inside the castle a warren of chambers and passageways can be explored. The castle was captured by 'Bonnie' Prince Charlie in 1745, and Mary, Queen of Scots was imprisoned here. Also here is the Museum of the Border Regiment. Its collection of weaponry, uniforms, medals and other personal items reveal many tragic and heroic stories from the wars in which the regiment has been involved.

In 1122, 30 years after the castle was built, Carlisle Cathedral was founded. It was originally a priory but became a cathedral under Henry I in 1132 and can claim to have held a daily service for almost 900 years. Inside, the first thing to strike the eye is the magnificent high ceiling. Its stained glass dates from the 14th to the 20th centuries – the oldest is in the East Window. Do not miss seeing the buildings opposite the cathedral's main entrance. The Fratry was a 13th-century monastic common room and now contains the cathedral library and the Prior's Kitchen Restaurant. Across from the Fratry, the 13th-century Prior's Tower was used, among other things, as a place of refuge from reivers and other Scottish raiders. Inside the tower, which can be seen by arrangement, is a ceiling with 45 panels, hand-painted in 1510.

Slightly overshadowed by the cathedral, but worth a visit, is St Cuthbert's Church, which was also built in the 12th century although the present buildings date from the 1700s. Its most unusual feature is a moveable pulpit, mounted on rail tracks, while the nearby tithe barn is now the church hall. This was used to house the tithes or taxes, paid in the form of wool, grain or straw.

CURSING STONE, CARLISLE MUSEUM

HADRIAN'S WALL

The city walls give some idea of the extent of the place in Roman times, as they were built – some 1,000 years after Hadrian's Wall – around the remains of the Roman town and fort. The West Walls, which run behind St Cuthbert's and around the cathedral, are the best surviving examples. These were begun in 1122 but not completed until 1200.

Carlisle's timber-framed Guildhall was built in 1404 and now houses the Guildhall Museum. Other notable buildings include the Citadel (a never-completed fortress begun in 1541) and the 18th-century Town Hall that is now a visitor centre.

HADRIAN'S WALL

In about AD 121, the Roman soldiers stationed in what became northern England began to build a wall that was to run for 73 miles (117.5km), from the Solway Firth to the River Tyne. Working under the instructions of the Emperor Hadrian (AD 76–138), the soldiers produced a barrier that would keep out the wild tribes of northern Britain, while Rome tried to civilise those behind the wall by introducing such features as central heating, public baths and an efficient drainage system.

There are several examples of such Roman remains at places along the Wall, though the finest examples – Chesters, Corbridge, Vindolanda and Housesteads – are to the east. In addition to the fort at Birdoswald, some parts of the western section of the Wall are worth visiting. There are the remains of turrets at Piper Sike, Leahill and Banks East, while at Hare Hill, near Lanercost, is a section of the Wall that stands some 9 feet (2.7m) in height.

The Wall now forms the western part of a UNESCO World Heritage Site – 'The Frontiers of the Roman Empire' – which includes large sections of Wall across Germany. The Hadrian's Wall Path National Trail between Bowness-on-Solway and Tynemouth opened in 2004 and is now one of England's most popular National Trails.

BEWCASTLE

CARLISLE & BORDERLANDS

TOURIST INFORMATION CENTRES

Brampton
Moot Hall, Market Square.
Tel: 01697 73433

Carlisle
The Old Town Hall.
Tel: 01228 625600

Gretna
Gretna Outlet Village.
Tel: 01461 337834

PLACES OF INTEREST

Bewcastle Cross
Bewcastle.

Birdoswald Roman Fort
Gilsland, near Carlisle.
Tel: 01697 747602
Dating from AD 125, the fort housed up to 500 Roman soldiers stationed on Hadrian's Wall. The perimeter wall, entrance gates and one turret can be seen. There is an interactive visitor centre on the site.

Border Regiment and King's Own Royal Border Regiment Museum
Queen Mary's Tower, The Castle, Carlisle. Tel: 01228 532774
Trophies, models, pictures and silver tell the story of the regiment.

Carlisle Castle
Castle Way, Carlisle.
Tel: 01228 591922
Medieval castle captured by 'Bonnie' Prince Charlie in 1745. Houses a regimental museum (see above).

Carlisle Cathedral
Tel: 01228 548151;
www.carlislecathedral.org.uk.
Founded in 1122, this handsome red sandstone church contains excellent stained glass and the Brougham Triptych – a 16th-century Flemish carved altarpiece.

Guildhall Museum
Green Market, Carlisle.
Tel: 01228 534781
Local history displays and the stories behind the Guilds.

Lanercost Priory
Tel: 016977 3030
Augustinian Priory in a delightful wooded valley 2 miles (3.2km) north-east of Brampton. The main priory buildings are in ruins, but the nave of the church survives and is now the local parish church.

Settle–Carlisle Railway
Scenic 72-mile (115.2km) route. For further details about the special steam trips which run occasionally along the line, as well as the standard trains, contact the local Tourist Information Centre or check the website www.settle-carlisle.co.uk.

Solway Aviation Museum
Carlisle Airport, Crosby-on-Eden.
Tel: 01228 573823;
www.solway-aviation-museum.co.uk
Exhibits include a Vulcan bomber as well as remnants from Blue Streak, the failed missile project from nearby RAF Spadeadam.

Tullie House Museum and Art Gallery
Castle Street, Carlisle.
Tel: 01228 534781
Interactive displays trace the history of Carlisle, including on the Romans, the reivers, Robert the Bruce and the Roundheads.

CARLISLE & BORDERLANDS

SHOPPING

Brampton

Market, Wed.

Carlisle

Market, Mon to Sat.

LOCAL SPECIALITIES

Ice creams and sorbets

Cumbrian Cottage, Gelt House Farm, Hayton, Carlisle.
Tel: 01228 670296

Woollens

Linton Tweed Shop (hand looms) Shaddongate, Carlisle.
Tel: 01228 527569

PERFORMING ARTS

Sands Centre

Carlisle. Tel: 01228 625222

Stanwix Arts Theatre

Brampton Road, Carlisle.
Tel: 01228 400300

SPORTS & ACTIVITIES

ANGLING

New Mills Trout Farm, near Brampton.
Tel: 01697 72384

Talkin Tarn Country Park

Tel: 01697 73129

CYCLE HIRE

Brampton

Pedal Pushers.
Tel: 01697 742387

GOLF COURSES

Brampton

Brampton Golf Club.
Tel: 01697 72255/72000

Carlisle

Carlisle Golf Club, Aglionby.
Tel: 01228 513303

Stony Holme, St Aidans Road.
Tel: 01228 625511

GUIDED WALKS

Carlisle

Guided city walks. Details from Carlisle Tourist Information Centre.

HORSE RACING

Carlisle Racecourse

Durdar Road.
Tel: 01228 522973

HORSE-RIDING

Brampton

Bailey Mill Farm, near Roadhead.
Tel: 01697 72384

Carlisle

Blackdyke Farm, Blackford.
Tel: 01228 674633
Cargo Riding Centre, Cargo.
Tel: 01228 674300
Stonerigg Riding Centre, The Bow, Great Orton.
Tel: 01228 576232

LONG-DISTANCE FOOTPATHS & TRAILS

The Cumbria Way

Carlisle and Ulverston are linked by this 70-mile (113km) route through the Lake District.

Hadrian's Wall National Trail

England's newest National Trail follows the Roman frontier for 84 miles (134km) from Bowness-on-Solway to Tyneside.

WATERSPORTS

Brampton

Talkin Tarn Country Park. Canoeing, rowing, sailing and windsurfing are available.
Tel: 01697 73129

ANNUAL CUSTOMS & EVENTS

Bewcastle

Bewcastle Sports (including sheepdog trials), late Aug.

Brampton

Brampton Sheepdog Trials, mid-Sep.

Carlisle

Carlisle and Borders Spring Show, early May.
Penton Sheepdog Trials, late May.
Carlisle Carnival, mid-Jun.
Cumberland Show, mid-Jul.

TEA ROOMS

The Boathouse Café

Talkin Tarn, Brampton,
CA8 1HN
Tel: 01697 73129

Upstairs from one of the tarn's boathouses, this welcoming café is the perfect place to reflect on the view and tuck into home-made cakes and hot chocolate. There's a little gift shop too.

Garden Restaurant

Tullie House Museum and Art Gallery,
Castle Street, Carlisle, CA3 8TP
Tel: 01228 534781
www.tulliehouse.co.uk

On the ground floor of the museum and art gallery, overlooking the quiet garden, this large refectory-style eatery is a great meeting place close to Carlisle's city centre. Serving snacks and more substantial lunches, it's also family friendly.

High Head Sculpture Valley Tearoom

High Head Farm, Ivegill,
Carlisle, CA4 0PJ
Tel: 016974 73552
www.highheadsculpturevalley.co.uk

Jonathan and Bernadette Stamper created this peculiar artistic haven on a working farm and the tea room is the ideal place to start or end your visit to the sculpture park. The exquisite food is freshly prepared, much of it following original farmhouse recipes, and the outside seating area offers glimpses into the sculpture park itself.

Castletown Farm Shop

Floriston Rigg, Rockliffe,
Carlisle
Tel: 01228 674400

Although adjacent to the motorway, and so not particularly scenic, this café and farm shop has built up a reputation for serving excellent locally sourced and organic food.

TALKIN TARN

Blacksmith's Arms
Talkin Village, Brampton, CA8 1LE
Tel: 01697 73452

This original smithy, dating from 1700, remains part of this attractive village inn standing in some of northern Cumbria's most scenic countryside. The Old Forge Restaurant's evenly balanced menu lists sweet and sour chicken, shepherd's and steak and kidney pie, spinach and ricotta cannelloni, fresh fillet of haddock and specialities such a beef stroganoff, loin of lamb and fresh salmon.

Crown Hotel
Wetheral, Carlisle,
CA4 8ES
Tel: 01228 561888
www.crownhotelwetheral.co.uk

Set in the attractive village of Wetheral and with landscaped gardens to the rear, this lovely hotel offers a relaxing atmosphere for hotel guests and non-residents. A choice of dining options are available, with the popular Waltons Bar an informal alternative to the main restaurant.

USEFUL INFORMATION

LAKE DISTRICT NATIONAL PARK INFORMATION POINTS

KENDAL, WINDERMERE & KENT ESTUARY

Elterwater
Maple Tree Corner Shop

Far Sawrey
The Post Office

Rusland
Forest Spinners

ESKDALE & WASDALE

Boot
The Post Office

Ravenglass
Ravenglass and Eskdale Railway Station

Ulpha
Ulpha Post Office, Duddon Valley, Broughton-in-Furness

Wasdale Head
Barn Door Shop

WESTERN LAKES

Ennerdale
Ennerdale Bridge Post Office

Gosforth
Gosforth Pottery

High Lorton
The Post Office

St Bees
The Post Office, 122 Main Street

ULLSWATER, PENRITH & EASTERN FELLS

Bampton
Bampton Post Office

PLACES OF INTEREST

We give details of just some of the facilities within the area covered by this guide. Further information can be obtained from local TICs or the web.

OTHER INFORMATION

Angling

Numerous opportunities for fishing on farms, lakes and rivers. Permits and licences are available from local tackle shops and TICs.

Cumbria Wildlife Trust

Plumgarths, Crook Road, Kendal.
Tel: 01539 816300;
www.wildlifetrust.org.uk

English Heritage

Canada House, 3 Chepstow Street, Manchester.
Tel: 0161 242 1400;
www.english-heritage.org.uk

Forestry Commission

Grizedale Forest Visitor Centre, Grizedale, Hawkshead, Ambleside.
Tel: 01229 860010

Lake District National Park Authority Headquarters

Murley Moss, Oxenholme Road, Kendal. Tel: 01539 724555;
www.lake-district.gov.uk

National Trust in Cumbria

The Hollens, Grasmere, Ambleside, Cumbria.
Tel: 0870 609 5391;
www.nationaltrust.org.uk

Parking

Information on parking permits and car parks in the area is available from local Tourist Information Centres.

Public Transport

The Traveline service gives details of buses, boats, trains and ferries operating throughout Cumbria.
Tel: 0870 608 2608

Weather

Lake District Weather Service.
Tel: 0870 055 0575

INDEX

Page numbers in **bold** refer to main entries.

ACKNOWLEDGEMENTS

The Automobile Association would like to thank the following photographers, companies and picture libraries for their assistance in the preparation of this book.

Abbreviations for the picture credits are as follows – (t) top; (b) bottom; (c) centre; (l) left; (r) right; (AA) AA World Travel Library.

2/3 AA/T Mackie; 5 AA/R Coulam; 6 AA/T Mackie; 9 AA/J Sparks; 12 AA/J Sparks; 13t AA/S Day; 13b AA/T Mackie; 14 AA/S Day; 15t AA/T Mackie; 15b AA/P Sharpe; 16 AA/T Mackie; 17 AA/S Day; 19 AA/A Mockford & N Bonetti; 20 AA/T Mackie; 23 AA/A Mockford & N Bonetti; 24/25 AA/A Mockford & N Bonetti; 26 AA/E A Bowness; 28/29 AA/J Sparks; 30 AA/S Day; 31t AA/T Mackie; 31b AA/P Sharpe; 33 AA/E A Bowness; 34/35 AA/A Mockford & N Bonetti; 38/39 AA/A Mockford & N Bonetti; 41 AA/A Mockford & N Bonetti; 42 AA/T Mackie; 44 AA/J Sparks; 46/47 AA; 48 AA/P Bennett; 50/51 AA/A Mockford & N Bonetti; 53 AA/S Day; 54/55 AA/A Mockford & N Bonetti; 57 AA/A Mockford & N Bonetti; 58/59 AA/S Day; 61 AA/A Mockford & N Bonetti; 63 AA/T Mackie; 64 AA/E A Bowness; 66 AA/E A Bowness; 70/71 AA/T Mackie; 73 AA/S Day; 79 AA/E A Bowness; 80 AA/C Lees; 82 AA/A Mockford & N Bonetti; 84/85 AA/T Mackie; 86 AA/J Sparks; 87 AA/A Mockford & N Bonetti; 88 AA/T Mackie; 89 AA; 90 AA/E A Bowness; 93 AA/A Mockford & N Bonetti; 94/95 AA/J Sparks; 97 AA/E A Bowness; 98/99 AA/J Sparks; 101 AA/T Mackie; 103 AA/E A Bowness; 106/107 AA/A Mockford & N Bonetti; 108/109 AA/T Mackie; 113 AA/A Mockford & N Bonetti; 115 AA/T Mackie; 116 AA/A Mockford & N Bonetti; 118 AA/T Mackie; 120/121 AA/J Sparks; 122 AA/P Sharpe; 123t AA/A Mockford & N Bonetti; 123b AA/A Mockford & N Bonetti; 125 AA/T Mackie; 126/127 AA/T Mackie; 128 AA/T Mackie; 130 AA/A Mockford & N Bonetti; 133 AA/E A Bowness; 134/135 AA/J Sparks; 138/139 AA/A Mockford & N Bonetti; 141 AA/A Mockford & N Bonetti; 147 AA/P Sharpe; 150 AA/S Day; 152/153 AA/T Mackie; 154 AA/S Day; 155 AA/T Mackie; 156 AA/A Mockford & N Bonetti; 157 AA/S Day; 158/159 AA/A Mockford & N Bonetti; 160 AA/E A Bowness; 162/163 AA/T Mackie; 165 AA/T Mackie; 166/167 AA/A Mockford & N Bonetti; 169 AA/T Mackie; 170 AA/A Mockford & N Bonetti; 173 AA/S Day; 174/175 AA/T Mackie; 177 AA/S Day; 183 AA/T Mackie; 184 AA/S Day; 186 AA/P Sharpe; 188/189 AA/E A Bowness; 190 AA/T Mackie; 191 AA/E A Bowness; 192 AA/A Mockford & N Bonetti; 193 AA/S Day; 194/195 AA/E A Bowness; 197 AA/S Day; 198 AA/E A Bowness; 201 AA/E A Bowness; 202/203 AA/E A Bowness; 204 AA/P Sharpe; 207 AA/E A Bowness; 208 AA/S Day; 210/211 AA/T Mackie; 213 AA/A Mockford & N Bonetti; 219 AA/T Mackie; 220 AA/A Mockford & N Bonetti; 222 AA/R Coulam; 224/225 AA/R Coulam; 226 AA/R Coulam; 227 AA/R Coulam; 228b AA/R Coulam; 228t AA/R Coulam; 229 AA/R Coulam; 231 AA/R Coulam; 233 AA/R Coulam; 234 AA/R Coulam; 237 AA/R Coulam; 238/239 AA/R Coulam; 241 AA/R Coulam; 247 AA/R Coulam; 248 AA/R Coulam

Every effort has been made to trace the copyright holders, and we apologise in advance for any accidental errors. We would be happy to apply the corrections in the following edition of this publication.